SHANGRI-LA
FOR
WOUNDED
SOLDIERS

SHANGRI-LA FOR WOUNDED SOLDIERS:

THE GREENBRIER AS A
WORLD WAR II ARMY HOSPITAL

LOUIS E. KEEFER

COTU PUBLISHING

First edition
4 3 2 1 95 96 97 98 99
ISBN: 0-9644740-0-X
Library of Congress Catalog No: 94-74604

Patient sketches by Robert Pearson Lawrence
Published by COTU Publishing
        P.O. Box 2160
        Reston, VA 22090-0160

Contents

Acknowledgments

This book has been a pleasure to write because the people who helped me — and there were a lot of them — have been wonderful to work with. More than a hundred are quoted and many more gave assistance. Without such help this book would not have been possible, so thanks to all of you.

Special thanks are owed to the dozen or so West Virginia newspaper editors who ran my author's query regarding Ashford General Hospital; Dr. Robert S. Conte, The Greenbrier's Historian, who allowed me to use the hotel archives and photographic collection; Lieutenant Colonel Iris J. West, AN, the Army Nurse Corps Historian, who shared with me certain material from the United States Army Nurse Corps Oral History Program, and who directed my attention to the Retired Army Nurse Corps Association; Martha McBroom, the National President of the Women's Army Corps Veterans Association, for the publication of a productive query in the association newsletter, *The Channel*; the editors of *The Retired Officer* magazine and the *West Virginia Disabled American Veterans Journal* whose publication of my queries generated additional responses; John A. Arbogast, a long-time White Sulphur Springs resident who described the town as it was before the war; Mary

Hanna, of Covington, Virginia, who gave me copies of her collection of the hospital's twice-a-month newspaper, *The Ashford News*; J.W. Benjamin, Jr., of Lewisburg who shared with me various photographs from his father's Ashford files; Dr. Richard J. Sommers, David Keogh, and John Slonaker of the Army Military History Institute; and the research librarians of the West Virginia State Archives.

My sincere thanks also to the three people who read the manuscript and gave me valuable suggestions for changes and clarifications: Dr. Robert S. Conte, Lt. Col. Iris J. West, and Dr. Ken Hechler, West Virginia's Secretary of State and World War II combat historian and author. Much is owed also to three steadfast but recognition-resistant helpers whose initials are A.B., L.J., and B.R.

1

The Hotel, The Town, and The Hospital

In 1940, White Sulphur Springs, West Virginia, was little more than an isolated crossroads on east-west U.S. Route 60. There were several small hotels, inns, and rooming houses, and the kinds of restaurants, stores, and services typical of a town of 2,000 people. Cradled deep in the Allegheny Mountains, in the southeastern corner of the state, White Sulphur Springs (until 1909, the village of Dry Creek) was rural, homey, and low-keyed.

Its famous and historic neighbor, The Greenbrier, was none of those things. The magnificent old resort was luxurious and sophisticated, a place where presidents and kings, the rich and the famous, and the scions of noted families came to relax or to amuse themselves. For over a century, The Greenbrier had offered its wealthy guests quiet elegance, grandeur, and tradition.

Though many residents of White Sulphur Springs worked in and around the hotel, they and the guests did not mingle. Guests and employees usually came from different social classes and had little in common.

A majority of the town's residents were descendants of Revolutionary War families and their ancestors came from

Scotland, Ireland, England, or northern Europe, but there were Italian, Greek, Middle Eastern, and Afro-American families as well. The admirable pictorial history, *Backward Glance: White Sulphur and Its People*, published by Debbie Schwartz Simpson (with John A. Arbogast), contains photographs of people with such surnames as Bowling, Cabell, Dameron, Easterly, Gillespie, Hicks, Justice, Loudermilk, McKenzie, O'Connell, Scott, and Wright. Though few townspeople were "well-off," few were poor. They ate simply, dressed conservatively, and a majority went to church on Sundays. White Sulphur Springs was a quiet, down-to-earth town, and its residents had every reason to expect that it would stay that way.

As different as they were, the worlds of the hotel and the town had a common origin: the spring of mineral water discovered in 1778 by the area's pioneer settlers. *The History of The Greenbrier: America's Resort,* by The Greenbrier's Historian, Dr. Robert S. Conte, provides a fascinating description of the long-term changes in the spa's social life:

> Southern aristocrats gathering about the Springhouse back before the Civil War engaged in politics, romance and "taking the waters"; beautiful and witty belles dancing at elaborate cotillions on summer evenings in the ballroom of the Old White Hotel; prominent high-society figures strolling into the Greenbrier's chandeliered dining rooms after stepping off their private railroad cars; presidents and professional golfers working on their best games against the legendary Sam Snead.

During this time span, the resort's name changed from "The Old White Hotel" to "The Greenbrier and Cottages," and at last to simply "The Greenbrier." In 1910, the Chesapeake and Ohio Railway bought the hotel and its grounds, and, starting in the late 1920s, began a dramatic expansion and renovation. The Virginia and North Wings were built, the number of rooms was doubled, the dining room was expanded to seat 650 people, and the hotel's interior was completely redecorated. A special siding for the railroad cars of VIP guests was added to the mainline C&O passenger station directly opposite The Greenbrier, and a private airport was built only two miles away. Three world-class golf courses were constructed.

Looking west from White Sulphur Springs beyond the hospital to the airport and prisoner of war camp at the foot of the mountains on the horizon, east-west U.S. Route 60 at lower left (Cummins Photo, courtesy Dr. Joseph Justo).

In earlier decades, seven American presidents and dozens of kings and queens were hotel guests. *The History of the Greenbrier* mentions just a few of the 1930's notables who came to the enlarged and refurbished resort:

David Sarnoff of RCA; Henry Luce, the publisher of *Life* magazine; Ham Fisher, the creator of "Joe Palooka"; New York Yankee Lou Gehrig; the "King of Jazz," Paul Whiteman; illustrator James Montgomery Flagg; Federal Relief Administrator Harry Hopkins; actress Mary Pickford; Babe Ruth, in his role as President of the Left-Handed Golfers Association; U.S. Steel President, Thomas Girdler; Eleanor Roosevelt; actor Edward G. Robinson; President of General Motors, William Knudsen; and singer Bing Crosby.

By 1940, The Greenbrier was really a self-contained city, offering splendid rooms, spacious public lounges, an air-conditioned theater, a magnificent indoor pool, and chic, expensive shops, all under one roof. The impressive main building was surrounded by acres of lawn and tree-shaded walks, and rows of guest cottages were spaced along paved roadways. The resort offered golf, tennis, skeet, riding, archery, and several other sports. Music, dancing, and new movies were available nightly. There was nothing to suggest that The Greenbrier soon would be caught up in events that would shatter its tranquillity for more than six years.

On December 17, 1941, just days after the Japanese attack on Pearl Harbor, the hotel's general manager received an urgent telephone call from the U.S. State Department. He was asked if the hotel would be willing to accommodate interned diplomats and citizens from the Washington embassies of hostile countries. The manager said it would, and within forty-eight hours, The Greenbrier no longer had or would accept regular guests.

According to *The History of the Greenbrier*, 159 Germans and Hungarians arrived in White Sulphur Springs by special train at 5:30 P.M. on the nineteenth of December. Others followed, and after four months The Greenbrier was home to over eight hundred diplomatic guests. Most were

German, but the total included 170 Italians, 53 Hungarians, and 11 Bulgarians. In addition to the diplomats and their families and servants, the internees included bankers, businessmen, journalists, military attachés, and engineers.

Townspeople viewed the Greenbrier's occupation by the enemy with something less than pleasure. The weekly *White Sulphur Springs Sentinel* reported outspoken criticism, and vigorous complaints soon forced authorities to hold a public meeting in nearby Lewisburg, the county seat. There, the Mayor of White Sulphur Springs, William Perry, reminded the crowd of its higher civic duty:

> Our whole tradition here in White Sulphur Springs is one of patriotism and support of our government. . . We, and I speak for every person in our town, are happy to have the privilege of doing our part during the war crisis.

Mayor Perry's speech, plus promises that the diplomats would be restricted to the hotel grounds and be under the constant surveillance of FBI agents and officers of the West Virginia State Police, seemed to settle the matter. At first, all Japanese diplomats were interned in the nearby Homestead Hotel in Hot Springs, Virginia. Then, mainly due to bickering between the Germans and the Italians, the non-Germans were transferred to another luxury hotel, the Grove Park Inn in Asheville, North Carolina, and the Japanese were moved from the Homestead to The Greenbrier. In her postwar book, *Bridge to the Sun*, Gwen Terasaki, the American wife of a Japanese diplomat, wrote about the move:

> We got settled at the Greenbrier with somewhat more ease than at the Homestead, and we found the Germans hospitable and glad to see us. There was much wining and dining and a number of gay cocktail parties among the higher ranking people of both embassies. . . . [On the other hand, because our bank accounts were frozen at first] we

had to be very thrifty to make our money last. I bought an ironing board and an electric iron and ordered a wooden drying rack from Sears, Roebuck and Co. Thus equipped, I proceeded to tackle the family wash. I am sure the elegant Greenbrier Hotel has never before or since had washing and ironing going on in so many of its luxurious rooms.

Within a few months, American and enemy diplomats began to be exchanged, and The Greenbrier's unique guests gradually departed. Over a nearly seven-month period, the hotel had hosted 1,697 people from five different nations. Though some had been arrogant and demanding, most had behaved responsibly, respecting the hotel's property and its staff. *The History of the Greenbrier* gives the following piece of information:

> On July 8, 1942, a final group of 151 German aviators left The Greenbrier and the resort's extraordinary 201 days of emergency government service came to an end. There was one interesting footnote: the German, Japanese, and Italian diplomats paid a total of $65,000 in gratuities to The Greenbrier's bellmen, maids, waiters, and porters for excellent services rendered.

The Greenbrier reopened to the public in mid-July, but its 1942 "season" lasted only six weeks. Even before the enemy diplomats departed, both the Army and the Navy had discussed with hotel management The Greenbrier's further use for wartime purposes. Both services expressed a keen interest, but the Navy wanted only about half the hotel's 650 rooms (allowing civilian use of the others), while the Army wanted to acquire the entire estate and to remake the hotel into a general hospital.

Something of an impasse between the services was broken in August 1942 by an arbitrating Army-Navy Board that ruled the Army's purpose should have priority. After the C&O and the Army failed to agree on a rental arrangement, the government condemned and bought the property under the War Powers Act. The C&O received $3.3 million for the hotel and 7,000 acres of West Virginia countryside, a package then thought to be worth at least $5.4 million.

The Greenbrier and several other resorts were acquired because the Army believed new hospitals could not be built quickly enough to accommodate future casualties. Anticipating reduced wartime patronage and probable operating losses, most managements readily agreed to sell or lease. Among the other resorts the Army purchased — none as famous as The Greenbrier — were the Don Cesar, St. Petersburg, Florida ($440,000); the Miami Biltmore, Coral Gables, Florida ($895,000); the Eastman, Hot Springs, Arkansas ($510,000); and the El Mirador, Palm Springs, California ($425,000).

In addition to its excellent physical facilities, The Greenbrier, a gleaming all-white structure in the Georgian-Colonial style, provided a beautiful and tranquil atmosphere for a hospital.* Though most of the wooden cottages predated the Civil War — one became the favorite postwar summer home of General Robert E. Lee — they proved great quarters for doctors and nurses. Trees and landscaped gardens were everywhere and, at 2,000 feet elevation, the resort remained cool even on summer nights.

The Army's arrival created headlines all over West Virginia and particularly in the town of White Sulphur Springs and in Greenbrier County. The weekly *Sentinel* proclaimed

---

* This was not the first time the resort was pressed into use as a hospital. At different times during the Civil War, both Union and Confederate forces employed then-existing buildings to treat the wounded. As a hospital, the original hotel buildings could accommodate as many as 1,600 patients, and archival records list the names of one hundred ninety-two Confederate soldiers who died there.

"Greenbrier Will Be Base Hospital," and suggested that many changes were sure to come. Some townspeople were surprised and concerned over the economic implications of this news, and feared the effect a large contingent of Army people might have on the community's daily life. They soon accepted, however, that the Army's arrival meant more jobs, more spending in local stores, and a unique opportunity for the town to contribute to the national war effort. After all, White Sulphur Springs had a long-standing and emotional connection to the Army. One of its citizens, Major General John L. Hines, had served with distinction in the Spanish-American War, the Philippine insurrection, and the First World War. He reached the top of his profession as the Army Chief of Staff from 1924 to 1926, the only West Virginian ever to hold that distinguished and powerful position.

Around the state, most West Virginians reacted positively to the Army's plans to make a hospital out of their well-known resort. An editorial in *The Charleston Gazette,* though incorrectly reporting that soldiers and sailors would share the facility, expressed the feelings of many Mountain State residents:

> All West Virginians feel a sort of proprietary interest in the Greenbrier. It is with distinct pride that we turn it over to our disabled soldiers and sailors and greet them with sincere hospitality and every wish for their quick recovery.

In the nation's capital, *The Washington Post* reported the sale, but was mistaken about the resort's intended use:

> Another casualty of World War II will be recorded in Washington this week as the Greenbrier Hotel in White Sulphur Springs, W.Va., a pleasure palace for 164 years, is officially turned over to the Government as a base for combat troops.

Once The Greenbrier's sale and the plans for the creation of a hospital were announced, the *Sentinel* reported all further news regularly — September 4, 1942: Greenbrier closed to guests, the Army prepares to move in; September 18, 1942: 2,000 new residents expected; 150 new homes required in the Villa Park addition; October 9, 1942: 350 local persons now employed; November 6, 1942: Hospital named Ashford General, medical staff continues to arrive; November 20, 1942: First patients come from New Jersey.

Beginning with its December 18, 1942 issue, the *Sentinel* maintained a regular column of "Hospital News," reporting major hospital events, as well as personnel promotions, reassignments, leaves, and even marriages. The hospital had replaced, and perhaps even surpassed, The Greenbrier as the town's center of attention. The hospital's new clientele — its sick and wounded soldiers — were, moreover, mostly just plain folks like the majority of the town's residents.

The Army rehired many former Greenbrier employees, and gave direct commissions to several key members of the management (including "old-timers" Roy B. Sibold, Robert A. Parker, and William Perry) as an inducement for them to remain at the hospital. This cadre of experienced hotel workers and managers, with their intimate knowledge of buildings and grounds, helped to ease the transition from hotel to hospital.

The demanding task of converting a 650-room hotel to a 2,000-bed hospital was accomplished surprisingly quickly. The first step was to dispose of equipment and furnishings the Army didn't want or need. Many veteran Greenbrier staff members were deeply disturbed over the fate of some hotel assets. As told in *The History of the Greenbrier* :

The [Army] policy was to retain only the most utilitarian kitchen equipment, linens, beds, chairs, and rugs. The hotel staff hastily removed the collection of historical books, photographs and valuable paintings from the Greenbrier and the President's Cottage Museum and loaned them indefinitely to nearby museums and universities. Other items were transferred to C&O Railway buildings. In the frantic rush to move out, there was neither time nor space to store the most expensive ornamental china, silver, lamps, furniture, prints, and mirrors. . . . the bulk of The Greenbrier's elaborate interior furnishings were quickly auctioned off at an unadvertised sale held at the White Sulphur Springs railroad station.

More than half a million dollars was spent on various physical changes. These included the creation on the fifth and sixth floors of a 600-bed surgical unit, with necessary temperature and humidity controls and special lighting. To move patients and equipment more speedily between floors, a massive elevator shaft was added to the front of the former hotel. Suites and rooms were reconfigured into thirty-nine wards, with thirty to sixty beds each. A dispensary, laboratory, dental clinic, post office, commissary, and post exchange (PX) replaced the shops in the lower lobby; the mineral baths area was designated as a center for hydrotherapy; the North Parlor was made into a chapel; the famous ballroom took on a new life as a recreation center filled with Ping-Pong tables. The log-constructed Kate's Mountain Lodge, overlooking the hospital from hundreds of feet above, became what many considered the Army's most beautiful Noncommissioned Officer's (NCO) Club. Many miles of bridle trails would remain, but the horses were moved to other locations, and the stables rebuilt inside for use as quartermaster warehouses.

Other projects included paving the ambulance driveway;

upgrading the sewage collection and disposal systems, the laundry, the kitchens, and the water treatment plant; building an on-site fire station; and converting the rows of summer cottages for year-round use. Later, it would be necessary to build barracks for Women's Army Corps (WAC) personnel, a Lester Building annex for certain civilian personnel, and a new recreation building.

This massive elevator shaft (right center) was added to the main building to accommodate the movement of patients, staff, and equipment between floors. Litter patients were brought here by ambulance (courtesy The Greenbrier).

One of the biggest projects was the construction, at the edge of the hotel's airport, of Camp Ashford, a 165-acre stockade for enemy prisoners of war (POWs). Work on the fifty-two building complex was begun during November 1942 and completed in May 1943. The prisoners were to maintain the hospital grounds, and perform the kinds of tasks that would free Army personnel for more important assignments. The first POWs — Italians captured in Tunisia —

did not arrive until six months after the hospital received its first patients. The Italians later were replaced by German POWs who remained for the duration of the war.

So much construction created something of an economic boom in White Sulphur Springs, and throughout southeastern West Virginia. Builders and workmen were attracted from up to two hundred miles away, and the new jobs drew under-employed men from small rural communities throughout the region.

The Ashford General Hospital was named in honor of Colonel Bailey K. Ashford (1873-1934).* Colonel Ashford graduated from Georgetown Medical School in 1896 and joined the Army Medical Corps a year later. He served in the first World War as Chief Surgeon for the Sixth Army Corps and was part of General Pershing's staff. Colonel Ashford achieved fame for the discovery of the intestinal hookworm that caused a vicious type of anemia that at one time ravaged the people of Puerto Rico.

The Army sent Colonel Clyde M. Beck of Memphis, Tennessee, to head the new hospital. The first doctor from that city to answer the call of duty in 1917, Colonel Beck was Assistant Division Surgeon with the 90th Division and served with distinction at the battle of the Meuse-Argonne. After service in the Philippine Islands, the Canal Zone, and at various posts in the United States, he was, just before his assignment to Ashford, the commanding officer of the station hospital at Camp Joseph T. Robinson, near Little Rock, Arkansas. An amiable "southern gentleman," and able administrator, Colonel Beck often was accompanied around the hospital by his Doberman pinscher, "Red."

---

* All but seven of the Army's sixty-six general hospitals in the United States were named for deceased Army officers; general hospitals overseas simply were numbered.

Colonel Beck's Executive Officer, the man who saw to it that orders were carried out, was Colonel Sam F. Seeley. A doctor himself, Colonel Seeley joined the Medical Corps in 1927 and served not only abroad, but at the Walter Reed Army Hospital in Washington, D.C. Before arriving at Ashford in September 1942, he had worked with the War Manpower Commission in that agency's managed allocation of doctors and dentists to armed forces versus civilian practice.

Most of Colonel Beck's senior staff, all highly qualified and experienced doctors, served at the hospital throughout the war. A surgeon since 1920, Colonel Daniel C. Elkin was Chief of the Surgical Service, the hospital's most important medical post. Before entering the Medical Corps in 1942, he had been Professor of Surgery and Chief Surgeon of the Emory University Hospitals.

Others among Ashford's top staff (as of January 1944) were Colonel Marshall Fulton, Chief of the Medical Service; Major Barnes Woodall, Chief of Neurological Surgery; Major Robert P. Kelly, Chief of Orthopedics; Major George C. Prather, Chief of the Urology Section; Major J.M. Masters, Chief of Ophthalmology; Major S.B. Kirkwood, Chief of the Women's and Officer's Section; Major E.N. Pleasants, Chief of the Neuropsychiatric Section; and Captain W.A. Galvin, Chief of Anesthesia and the Operating Room Section.

During the course of the war, several hundred Army doctors, dentists, and nurses served at Ashford, many before serving overseas, and others after having done so. The numbers and specialities of the medical staff varied with the number of patients and with the types of wounds and illnesses. At the beginning of the war, and again near its end, the staff had less hectic schedules, but during the years of the heaviest fighting, work continued at top speed. The early years saw more patients needing surgery, while in later years more of them required treatment for skin and intestinal problems.

As the hospital staff expanded during the late months of 1942, uniformed men and women began to be seen in various White Sulphur Springs shops and restaurants. Some people maintained an initial reserve toward the senior officers, uncertain about the protocol for meeting and dealing with them, but younger officers and enlisted men were accepted into the community almost as if they had grown up there. In many ways, they became substitutes for the town's own young men and women who had gone into the armed forces.

Ashford General Hospital began its official functions on November 20, 1942, when the first trainload of wounded men arrived after processing at the Tilton General Hospital in New Jersey. Many had come from Guadalcanal, the Aleutian Islands, or North Africa. Since the Army's usual practice was to send men to hospitals near their homes, many of the patients were from Virginia, West Virginia, Ohio, and other nearby states. In the years that followed, more than 24,000 patients — distinguished by their maroon pajamas and robes — were treated at Ashford, the hospital that journalists and many other people soon began calling "a Shangri-La for sick and wounded soldiers."

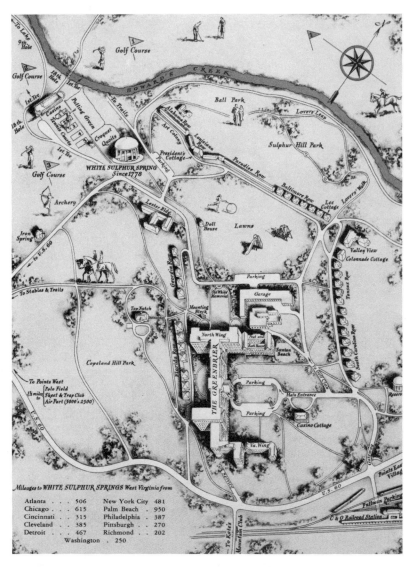

This plan of The Greenbrier buildings and grounds was part of a four-page brochure given to patients and staff as they arrived at Ashford General Hospital. The town of White Sulphur Springs lay just to the east along U.S. Route 60; Charleston, the capitol of West Virginia (omitted from the legend), lay about 100 miles to the west-northwest; Richmond, Virginia, 202 miles to the east.

PFc JOHN HALL JR
31776302

WARD 601 ASHFORD
GENERAL HOSPITAL
WHITE SULPHUR SPRINGS
WVA.

ROBERT F LAWRENCE
SKETCHED UNDER THE SPONSORSHIP
OF USO CAMP SHOWS. INC. JULY 9 44

2

Patients: The Men In Maroon

During World War II, the stateside general hospital usually was the last stop in the chain of evacuation from the field first-aid station through the U.S. Army Medical Department's "full course of repair." Such repair aimed first at quickly returning men to active duty. The alternative was to treat them and send them home as whole as possible.

Life magazine for January 29, 1945, traced the 4,500-mile evacuation odyssey of infantryman George Lott in a series of now-famous photographs. Eight distinct moves were documented:

Wounded by mortar fragments in both arms, Lott walked to his battalion aid station, where his shattered arms were put in traction splints and he was given morphine, blood plasma, and sulpha tablets. (2) When German shellfire let up, he was taken by ambulance to a collecting station ten-minutes away. (3) He then was moved another fourteen-miles back from the front to a clearing station equipped for major first aid and emergency surgery. There he was cleaned up, doctors gave him new splints and dressings, and (4) he was sent further back to an evacuation hospital, reaching it six hours and ten minutes after his wounding.

After a difficult three-hour operation, and immobilization in a body cast to prevent any arm movements, Lott spent four days in the evacuation hospital, before (5) being flown to a base hospital in England. A day later, a hospital train took him to (6) the 7th General Hospital near London where he had a further operation and received a fresh body cast. (7) Lott was flown home to Mitchel Field*, New York, a month after his wounding, and (8) later moved to the Rhoads General Hospital in Utica, New York — his last stop and close to home.

Ashford was a major center for two specialities: vascular surgery and neurosurgery. In addition to patients arriving directly from the war zones — many of whom made longer and more painful journeys to reach America than did George Lott — Ashford also received patients assigned for special treatment by other general hospitals in the United States. Some emergency patients, taken seriously ill while on leave, or injured in training, arrived from towns in West Virginia and Virginia.

Frank E. Funk, from North Little Rock, Arkansas, was one of Ashford's first patients. He entered the Army in June 1939 and was among the original cadre of the 1st Armored Division Combat Command B, one of the first American ground forces to reach Europe. During manuevers in northern Ireland, his tank threw a tread and turned over. As the tank's commander, 1st Sgt. Funk stayed inside to turn off its master switches, and to remove live 37mm shells. When one exploded in his hand, he was pulled from the tank with

---

* Named not for the famous flyer General "Billy" Mitchell, but for John P. Mitchel, mayor of New York City (1913-17), who in 1918 volunteered for the Army Air Service, and was killed in an airplane crash in Louisiana.

his uniform in flames and sped by ambulance to the 5th General Hospital in Belfast. There he lost two fingers and spent three days in intensive care before returning to the U.S. by hospital ship:

"When I first got back, I was temporarily hospitalized at Fort Dix, New Jersey. I didn't know it, but my wife had come to Fort Dix after I was already on my way to West Virginia. I'd just settled into my room at Ashford when a nurse came and said 'Your wife's here in the lobby waiting to see you.' I said 'Oh no, my wife's back in Arkansas. She doesn't even know I'm here.' But I went down, and there she was! They'd told her at Fort Dix where I was going. That was Christmas Day, 1942, and what a glorious day it was!

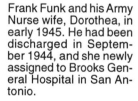

Frank Funk and his Army Nurse wife, Dorothea, in early 1945. He had been discharged in September 1944, and she newly assigned to Brooks General Hospital in San Antonio.

"I was at Ashford until April 6, 1943. I was assigned to the neurological ward where I had seven operations. The doctors and nurses were wonderful. After leaving Ashford, I remained in the Army until my discharge in September 1944. I received a thirty per cent disability (now, I'm rated ninety per cent disabled). I re-enlisted after the war, and retired in 1962 with twenty-two years of service."

The Hotel Hart was always full (courtesy Jack Carte).

Hospital visitors such as Frank Funk's wife, Dorothea, could stay at any of several hotels, motels, and rooming houses in the White Sulphur Springs area. While Ashford General was in operation, most of them did a booming business. The largest hotels were the Hart, the West Virginia, and the Alvon. The Hart, a handsome old two-story structure with a sloping tin roof and sheltering elm trees, advertised rooms at, "Single, $1.50 and up," or "Double, $2.00 and up."

Day after day, families and friends arrived for visits. In three and a half years, there were more than 50,000 of them. All hospital visitors, including volunteer workers and entertainers, were admitted to the grounds at an entrance guarded by military police (MPs). Many came on foot, because of parking restrictions. Visitors arriving by car were subject to a strictly enforced 15 mph speed limit.

James Thomas ("Tommy") Miller was born in the little town of Hico, West Virginia. Drafted in 1943, he was with the 79th Infantry Division when it came ashore at Omaha Beach on June 9, 1944. Less than a month later, while fighting outside St. Lo with a heavy weapons platoon, Cpl. Miller was hit "all up and down my back" with fragments from a German 88. His left hip joint was smashed, and his left ankle badly lacerated:

"After they got me back to the field hospital, they cut me open from just below my neck clear down to my groin to take out shrapnel. When I woke up several days later, I had been shot so full of ether that it almost got me. After I became fully conscious, my left leg still hurt terribly. They put it into a cast that I wore for nine months.

"From France, they flew me in a C-47 litter-plane to a base hospital in the U.K. There I was put aboard a four-engined C-54, and flown, via Newfoundland, back to Mitchel Field on Long Island. My brother, who was posted there, came for a visit but didn't even recognize me. Still in my cast, I was put on another C-47 and flown to White Sulphur Springs. The grass runway was just a cow pasture, and soldiers were posted there to keep the cattle off.

"Meanwhile, inside the cast, my hip became infected. They could probably have smelled me all over the hospital. Even after the infection was cleared up with penicillin and some sulpha drugs, I almost lost my leg. They started to take it off three times, but finally they never did. They said I'd never walk on it, but even though I have had to use crutches and canes ever since, I managed to walk out of Ashford under my own power.

"My cast had to be changed several times while I was there, and after four months or so, they put a leg iron on it so I could get around a little. My parents drove down, and took me home for Christmas 1944. I sprawled stiff-legged across the back seat, and the fifty-mile drive wasn't bad.

Men in wheelchairs raced down this sloping walk from the hospital past the Springhouse to the Casino (Cummins Photo, courtesy Dr. Joseph Justo).

"There were always a lot of entertainers coming and going around the hospital. Walter Pidgeon was there. I really liked that man! He played some five-card draw poker with us one night. He seemed like just a beginner, and I won thirty-three dollars from him. Short on cash, he wrote me a check. Esther Williams was there, too. She gave swimming lessons in the hospital's indoor pool and helped men who were there for water therapy. Once, after I'd guided my wheelchair down the special ramp into the water, she helped me free of it. She was very beautiful.

"Some of us were crazy enough to race against each other in our wheelchairs, down that long hill from the north entrance of the hospital to the golf clubhouse, or the Casino as most people called it. Nice wide sidewalks curved down past the Springhouse, and it didn't seem dangerous, just something to do. They had this rear-loading van they'd bring down to take us back to the top again. We could also go to town and back in it. Once I went down to the Pines, a small nightclub west of town on U.S. Route 60, and I attended some free movies in the hospital theater, but I didn't do much letter writing or reading."

After the invasion of Europe, more and more wounded soldiers (like Cpl. Miller) were flown back home instead of being put on increasingly crowded hospital ships. Even within the United States itself, railroad traffic congestion dictated that more and more wounded be moved by air. The C-47 and the C-54 air ambulances used for these purposes were converted twin-engined Douglas DC-3s and four-engined Douglas DC-4s. The planes flew below 9,000 feet and some flights were bumpy. The C-47 could carry eighteen patients in three tiers of canvas stretchers. The C-54 could carry about twice as many. Army "flight" nurses accompanied each plane, administering treatments as required. To better serve the patients brought to Ashford, the grass cow pasture airstrip was replaced with a paved 3,500-foot runway capable of supporting planes weighing up to 15,000 pounds.

Stuart Eisenberg was completing his internship at a hospital in New York City when he was drafted. Assigned as its medical officer, he landed with the 757th Light Tank Battalion at Casablanca in 1943. Moved up the Moroccan coast to Port Lyautey, the 757th spent six months with an infantry regiment that was guarding the Allied left flank against any surprise German attack via Spain and across the Strait of Gibraltar. While at Port Lyautey, it was one of Eisenberg's duties to accompany enlisted men going to Fez for rest and relaxation and to run a prophylactic station for men visiting the brothels. Just before his unit was moved to Tunisia in preparation for the invasion of Italy, Eisenberg contracted poliomyelitis:

"I was hospitalized in North Africa for about a month, then came home on the *Pacific Queen,* a big liner-turned-troopship fitted out with a hospital section. We landed in New York. From there, I came down by hospital train through Washington to Richmond, and then on to White Sulphur Springs. That was about November 1943. I remember, because it was snowing like crazy. I was at Ashford through 1944 and most of 1945, about twenty-two months.

"It was a long-term care sort of thing, and I achieved only a partial recovery. I was given different kinds of physical therapy, including the regular use of the swimming pool, for nine months before they tried to put me on my feet. I had to be lifted from my bed into my wheelchair. Then they'd wheel me down a special ramp into the pool, where I could roll off right into the water. Gradually they got me up on leg braces and crutches.

"I was very impressed with the doctors there, and with the commanding officer, Colonel Beck. Even Hollywood would have thought him the very epitome of a high-ranking officer: he dressed impeccably, always had his Doberman pinscher at his heels, and sometimes even carried a riding crop. He always acted in a most correct military way.

"As a doctor myself, sometimes I was allowed to attend staff meetings. The mostly young and very bright doctors would ask Colonel Beck to join them, and often would invite his advice on some point or other. He would say, 'No, no, gentlemen. I have no comments. Carry on as before.' I never heard of any staff complaints. I don't know how good Colonel Beck was as a doctor, but he was clearly a fine hospital administrator.

First Lieutenant Stuart Eisenberg, M.D., on the circular driveway that looped around to Ashford's main entrance.

"They did everything they could to keep us happy. I went to the movies a lot. And I remember one really terrific Red Cross volunteer who would give us back rubs, do errands, and even take three or four of us out for dinners at restaurants downtown. She also took us for car rides through the beautiful West Virginia hills sometimes.

"My parents came to see me a couple of times, staying at a motel, and my wife-to-be also visited several times. I saw Ed Wynn and Esther Williams when they entertained.

Williams spoke to everyone. 'Hi there, soldier. How're you doin'? What's your name? Where're you from?' She carried photos of herself, and signed one for me reading, 'To Stuart, with love, Esther Williams.'"

Stuart Eisenberg with his fiancée, Sylvia Sidenberg, on the Casino patio, early 1945

Comedian Ed Wynn, "The Perfect Fool," and his USO troupe did stage shows at Ashford on March 15th and 16th in 1944. Wynn, aged fifty-eight, had starred in the "Ziegfield Follies of 1914," and became famous in the thirties, wearing a red fire hat as the Texaco Fire Chief. Actress-singer Wini Shaw and accordionist Michael Olivieri accompanied Wynn as he visited every hospital ward, bantering, singing, and playing for the patients. Wynn and Shaw gave autographs and shook hands with each man.

The indoor swimming facility so well remembered by such patients as Stuart Eisenberg was the magnificient 100' by 42' mosaic-tiled pool presided over by Charles Norelius. A three-time Swedish swimming champion, Norelius was for many years the hotel's swimming coach. Ideal for use in physical therapy, the pool was enjoyed by patients and post personnel alike. Swim suits were available at no charge.

Film star Esther Williams performed one of her famous water ballets at the pool. The talented film star — all 5'7" and 123 pounds of her — was a great success. Not only did she swim but she sang a few ballads for the capacity crowd of several hundred men. She visited the wards, signed leg and body casts, lunched in the patients' mess hall, and chatted with dozens of men in the Red Cross Recreation Hall.

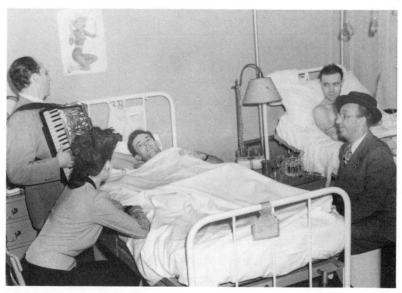

USO troupers Wini Shaw, Ed Wynn, and Michael Olivieri entertained patients in their rooms. Western style "pin-ups" such as that tacked to the wall were very popular (courtesy J.W. Benjamin, Jr.).

"Splash parties" were inaugurated in January 1945, and soon became a weekly affair. They featured competitive races and water games, but the main idea was to have fun: "hostesses" in bathing suits, "rug cutting" to live dance music, and the Red Cross snack bar all made for high morale. By September 1945, elaborate shows were being performed by post personnel and volunteers. "The Legend of the South Seas" featured the local high school swimming star, Alice Carte, as a beautiful princess rescued by a charming prince, played by Sgt. Walter Hazeltine of the Special Service unit. Young Donna Kerkam, Col. Beck's granddaughter, was also a member of the cast.

The start of a "Splash Party" (courtesy The Greenbrier).

One of the men who ultimately would benefit greatly from the therapeutic power of the swimming pool was Roger B. Judkins, a 1942 graduate of the University of New Hampshire. Having been in the Reserve Officer Training Corps (ROTC), he needed only a refresher course at Fort Benning, Georgia, to get his commission. Assigned to the 2nd Infantry Division, he led an 81mm mortar platoon advancing on St. Lo through the hedgerow country of Normandy. The platoon was near St. Georges D'Elle when a German shell exploded in the trees overhead, killing several of his men, and spraying him with shrapnel:

"A litter case, I was first flown to England, then back to the U.S. and White Sulphur Springs. A number of operations were performed to find and repair the nerve damage that had caused my left leg to be paralyzed from the knee down. The doctors also continued to remove the shrapnel, and to clean up my other wounds. By the late fall of 1944, I could use a wheelchair, and was on crutches in time to take Christmas leave in New York. They continued to give me whirlpool baths and pool therapy until April 1945, when I went home for good.

"Sometimes, while we were reading the newspapers, the German POWs would come to clean our rooms and they'd see photographs from the war zone showing Germans surrendering in droves (this was in early 1945). Although they couldn't read English, they knew exactly what was going on, and hoped the war would end soon, so they could go home. They were all over the place, even in downtown White Sulphur Springs. You could go into a gas station and there'd be guys with the big white 'PWs' painted everywhere on their uniforms, trustees I suppose.

"Right after one of my operations, a German was shot, and he was brought into a room near mine. All of the nurses ran in there to see the 'superman.' That was big stuff, and I had a helluva time getting what I needed. It's a good thing my wife had moved to White Sulphur Springs and was there in the recovery room with me. She went and got help when I had to have it. Despite this one instance, I'd have to say that I had excellent treatment throughout my stay. Ashford was the absolutely best place in the world for rehabilitation and getting to feel right again."

Though Camp Ashford, the prisoner of war enclosure at the airport, was built to the standard Army design capable of holding 1,000 men, it probably never did. Near the end of the war, 679 German POWs lived in the camp, and worked at Ashford, but 253 had been assigned to the Newton D. Baker General Hospital in Martinsburg, West Virginia, while 41 others worked and were housed in a lumber camp near East Rainelle, West Virginia. Both of the latter locations were considered "branch camps" to Camp Ashford's "base camp." Prisoners weren't required to work outside the base camp, but, in accordance with the Geneva Convention, they could do so voluntarily for extra pay.

Charles W. Conner, from the Charleston, West Virginia area, was with the 116th Regiment, 29th Infantry Division when he was hit by mortar fire a week after D-Day. After emergency treatment, Sgt. Conner was flown to England, then put aboard the *Blanche S. Sigman,* an Army hospital ship named in memory of an Army nurse killed on the Anzio beachhead. Because of a breakdown in the mid-Atlantic, the ship took sixteen days to reach Charleston, South Carolina. Conner was taken to White Sulphur Springs by hospital train, and would stay at Ashford for almost two years:

"I had many operations, and I think the doctors and nurses were the greatest, especially Major Robert Kelly, Chief of Orthopedics. I had already been up on crutches by the time I got to Ashford and I was getting around better and better. At one point I met Sam Snead and had a try at golf, playing on crutches the first hole of the nine-hole course reserved for beginners like me.

"My parents came up to see me sometimes, driving up and back the same day. They were impressed that I had what was called the 'King George Room.' I didn't go to the movies nor do I recall seeing any of the USO shows. I did go to the Casino now and then, and into White Sulphur Springs for some meals. Being at Ashford was a good experience, the best hospital I've ever known."

Not only did some men play golf on crutches, others played with an arm or leg missing. A tournament for patients who had the use of only one hand attracted forty-five entrants. The winner, Pfc. Edward Mahaffey, got an engraved silver cup and a wallet. The runners-up were Pfc. Frank Kozibroda and Pvt. Gene Dunne. Major Theodore D. Chrimes, the head of the hospital's reconditioning section made the awards in the War Department Theater, the new name for the large auditorium in the main building.

For men who had never played before, informal golf lessons and some starting tips were available from Special Service's Cpl. Peter S. Petroske, once the professional at the Meriden Country Club in Connecticut. The sport was so popular that Col. Beck, an avid golfer, found it necessary to issue rules and regulations on golf etiquette. Due to a wartime scarcity of rubber, all balls were reconditioned, and cost a quarter, but were only "on loan, to be returned after play." Even so, Col. Beck's rules reminded players, "GOLF BALLS ARE SCARCE! DON'T LOSE THEM! And DON'T DRIVE THEM OVER WATER HAZARDS!" Though patients could borrow clubs at no charge, post personnel had to buy season memberships: officers paid $5; sergeants, $3; other enlisted men, $2. Civilians needed special passes to play, and had to furnish their own equipment and golf balls.

Robert C. Wasson, born near Pittsburgh, Pennsylvania, had an advanced degree in economics when he went to work at the War Industries Board in Washington, D.C. Drafted into the Army in March 1942, he was questioned about his allergy problems, but denied the possibility that

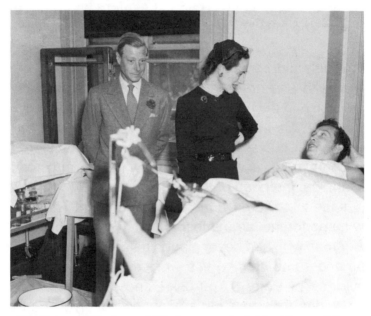

The Duke and Duchess of Windsor came to Ashford General Hospital in October 1943 and visited with many men in their rooms (courtesy J.W. Benjamin, Jr.).

they might restrict his Army service. He finished basic training with the 90th Infantry Division, and then completed Officer Candidate School (OCS) at Fort Benning, Georgia. Several assignments later, he was sent to the South Pacific theater, where he joined the Tenth Corps headquarters company as Personnel Officer:

"I went first with the 88th Infantry Division to New Guinea, serving as both Executive Officer and Personnel Officer, and subsequently took part in the Leyte and Mindanao landings in the Philippines. Before going to Japan in September 1945, I was transferred into the 8th Army headquarters as Assistant Information Officer, and promoted to captain.

"Shortly after arriving in the Pacific, my skin problems flared up. The medics gave me lotions, which only worsened my condition. Finally, at a hospital in Tokyo, the doctor called my condition pre-cancerous and sent me home. In San Francisco, I boarded a crowded hospital train that dropped patients at stops all the way to West Virginia.

"I think it was Christmas Eve of 1945 when we arrived at the hospital, with lots of snow around, and everything decorated for the holidays. There I found a doctor who knew something about my particular skin problem. His opinion was that I had been over-medicated. He cut off the pills and lotions and my skin eventually cleared up by itself. The culprit was likely the Atabrine I took to prevent malaria. 'Tokyo Rose' used to say taking it would make a man impotent, but, of course, the enemy just hoped we'd not take the medicine then get malaria and become too sick to fight. The Army knew about Atabrine's side effects and the Germans, who discovered it before World War I, were certainly aware of them."

After the war, Capt. Wasson was assured by an Army medical historian that a recognition of the drug's side effects had been restricted because of a feared increase in refusals to take it. Eventually, an officer was directed to be present at one meal a day to guarantee that every enlisted man took his pills. In fact, one of Wasson's duties had been to see that all 10th Corps officers enforced the rule.

The "Tokyo Rose" Robert Wasson mentions was no single person as her G.I. radio listeners generally believed, but a number of different Japanese women with similarly seductive voices. Both of America's major enemies were adept at psychological warfare. The broadcasts of "Tokyo Rose" and "Axis Sally," her American-born counterpart in Berlin,* were meant to sap the morale of Allied fighting men. Most American servicemen found these broadcasts somewhat amusing, knowing them to be propaganda, but many men still believed that Atabrine would make them impotent, and they tried to avoid taking it.

Calvin White grew up near Charleston, West Virginia, and had spent two years in the Civilian Conservation Corps before he was drafted in 1941. He reached the South Pacific in March 1942, was there for twenty-eight months, and, toward the end of that period, served in the Americal Division. Two months after returning to the States, Sgt. White suffered a malaria attack while home on leave, and was rushed by Army ambulance ("the roughest ride I ever had") to White Sulphur Springs:

"They put me in a room on the second floor with seven other men, all of us with malaria. We were so crowded, you could barely squeeze between the beds. We got four or five pills at a time, three times a day, varying quinine and Atabrine. Five or six doctors would come in together to check on how we were doing. We were like guinea pigs. They wouldn't let us leave the room, and I stayed there eighteen days. It got so tiresome, I opened the window to get out on the balcony, but somebody noticed, and they made me get back in bed. We didn't have any civilian visitors, either, not even any Red Cross people. We were virtually quarantined.

"The funny thing is I'd never had malaria in the Pacific,

* "Axis Sally" was Mildred Gillars of Columbus, Ohio, who was convicted of treason and sentenced to a long term in a federal penitentiary in Alderson, West Virginia, less than thirty miles from White Sulphur Springs.

so when I got sick, I didn't know what was wrong with me. I was waiting for a bus to go to Charleston when I started feeling funny, and my fingertips turned numb. During the trip, the numbness seemed to move all the way up my arm, and I started to chill, and shake, and ache all over. When we got to town, the bus driver and two soldiers helped me to a dispensary in the basement of the Kanawha Hotel, where a Navy pharmacist's mate took one look at me and said I had malaria.

"That corpsman could tell I'd been in the Pacific and taking Atabrine because of how yellow I was. He said that we were supposed to keep taking Atabrine for six months after coming home, but nobody had ever told me that, or given me a supply to bring home. Even after I left Ashford, I probably had malarial attacks fifteen or twenty times for about three years. I took Atabrine, which the Veterans Administration supplied free, until 1957."

William S. Crumlish of Pleasant Gap, Pennsylvania, was on Guadalcanal when he developed a severe case of dermatitis — commonly called "jungle rot" — all over his legs, feet, and back. When the pain became so bad that Capt. Crumlish could no longer walk, he was ordered to the 52nd Field Hospital on Bougainville. He was later returned to Guadalcanal, to the 137th Station Hospital, then to the 24th General Hospital at Nouvea, New Caledonia, and finally was sent to the U.S. on a hospital ship. After a week at Letterman General Hospital in San Francisco, he came by hospital train to Ashford General, arriving March 8, 1945:

"At the hospital on Guadalcanal, they dunked my whole body up to my chin in potassium permanganate three times a day. When I went to the 24th General Hospital on New

Caledonia, they said I had been 'over-medicated,' and that they would employ a program of 'skillful neglect,' meaning soaks in mild boric acid solution, and plenty of good food and rest. 'We'll just try to ease your pain, and let mother nature do her thing.' The doctors there also used X-ray treatment on my infected legs before sending me back to the States.

"Tropical dermatitis was really serious stuff, potentially fatal. One of my roommates at Letterman died of it my second night there. But I was lucky, and by the time I got to White Sulphur Springs, I was just about ambulatory. The hospital was such a wonderful change from the jungle. I'd sit in the post exchange and eat ice cream, then go around admiring the beautiful chandeliers in the lobby and dining room. I was awestruck just to be back in civilization.

"I didn't participate in sports at Ashford, and didn't get into town. I don't remember the USO shows or anything like that, either. I was entirely focused on getting well. I do recall seeing the German POWs. They did a great job keeping the grounds looking like a well-groomed city park. Within a few weeks, I was allowed to go home on a convalescent leave. From then on, my time was divided between home and hospital until I was released to resume limited duty. Everybody who was connected with treating wounded soldiers, both overseas and in the U.S., deserves to be commended. They all earned my highest respect."

Later in the war, as more and more men served in the South Pacific, one of Ashford's busiest sections was Dermatology. The large number of men then arriving with skin diseases, many of them unknown to American doctors, was responsible for a significant shifting of the hospital's resources. The Dermatological Section, then headed by Lt.

Col. Herbert L. Traenkle, was given the hospital's entire fourth floor and doctors and nurses were reassigned as needed.

William E. Leopold, from Jim Thorpe, formerly Mauch Chunk, Pennsylvania, was wounded by machine gun fire on January 22, 1945, near Maldingen, Belgium, while serving as first scout in Company C, 291st Regiment, 75th Infantry Division. Pfc. Leopold's ammunition belt and uniform caught fire, and his life was in jeopardy until his lieutenant, Mathew M. Labuz, crawled to him and smothered his burning clothes with snow. The lieutenant then dragged him to safety inside a barn, where Leopold endured the night with frostbitten toes, and stomach and leg wounds:

"I spent a long time in field hospitals in Paris and then in England, arriving back home by hospital ship on May 5, 1945. I was at the Halloran General Hospital on Staten Island, New York, for only a few days, then was asked what hospital I'd like to go to next. I told them Valley Forge, which was the closest to home, but I was sent to Ashford instead.

"It hardly seemed like an Army hospital, and my stay there was very nice. I had one serious operation, and felt that all the doctors and nurses were great. Several had already served overseas, and had been rotated home. They knew what it was all about.

"After a while, I could get around in a wheelchair, and I enjoyed coasting down the sidewalk to the PX in the Casino, having a beer or two, and listening to the jukebox. Coming back up the hill was the hard part. I had to wait for some good samaritan to push me.

"Every Sunday, the Army band would play out in front of the hospital, and in the evenings some of us just sat around in the lobby watching people go by. My father and mother came down by train to see me a few times, and I attended lots of movies and shows. Robert 'Believe-It-Or-Not' Ripley came into my room and had a photo taken with one of my roommates. When I could manage crutches, I'd follow one of the walking trails and sit on a bench overlooking a part of the town. I passed many a pleasant evening there.

Pfc. William Leopold enjoys the West Virginia sunshine.

"I left Ashford on January 23, 1946, after being there some eight months. I came out using a cane. Now I walk with two canes or crutches and I'm rated as totally disabled. My wife and I visited the Greenbrier in 1990 and the memories came flooding back, especially that of Christmas 1945 — a far cry from my Christmas 1944 in Belgium."

Men in wheelchairs or on crutches had easy accessibility to numerous walking paths on the hospital grounds. One of the more gentle paths, "Lovers Walk," led to "Lovers Leap,"* a point high above Howard's Creek, with a broad view of White Sulphur Springs. While much of the downtown sprawled out on relatively level land, the hospital and its grounds were located atop the somewhat higher rolling hills just to the west.

Renardo J. Della Rocca, from Brooklyn, was drafted April 11, 1941, graduated from OCS, and eventually became an infantry platoon leader with the Americal Division. Wounded in both legs by Japanese grenades and small arms fire, he went back through battalion aid to an evacuation hospital and then to the 31st General Hospital at Espiritu Santo. From there, he was shipped to Letterman General Hospital in San Francisco, and to Boston's Cushing General Hospital.

"They didn't know what to do with me at Cushing. There was a lot of pain in both legs, and it seemed neurological.But then they found what they called 'arteriovenous fistulae' in first one leg then the other. Some major veins and arteries in my legs somehow had grown together, 'short-circuiting' my blood circulation before it reached my feet. I had surgery to separate the blood vessels, and tie them off where they'd joined. The doctors said that if they didn't do that, there was some danger of my heart becoming dangerously enlarged by having to pump too hard.

* Legend has it that Lovers Walk led to "Courtship Maze," at the end of which was a crucial juncture: to the left was "Rejection Row," a dead end into the woods, while on the right was "Acceptance Way to Paradise," a path leading to Paradise Row, whose cottages often were used by honeymooners.

The Springhouse following a heavy snow (courtesy Clint Beuscher).

"At Letterman I had been repaired enough to walk, but after the surgery at Ashford I made more rapid progress. My wife came down, and the Red Cross helped her find a room in town. She was there all the time I was in the hospital. We often had dinner in a restaurant that offered good southern fried chicken and were surprised at the number of people drinking champagne in a state that was supposed to be 'dry.' I guess no one would arrest some decorated veteran.

"The hospital was a grand place. My wife and I used to walk around the grounds, and from the golf clubhouse we could sit and watch the golfers and the swans on the nearby lake. An occupational therapist taught me how to model in clay and to weave, and she was terrific. I always think of Ashford as a kind of a dream I'd like to return to — maybe play a round or two of golf. I sure was happy there."

Charles L. Colvin of Belpre, Ohio (near Parkersburg, West Virginia), was drafted on January 29, 1941. Following the Japanese attack on Pearl Harbor, his 1291st Task Force was sent to protect the oil refineries on Curacao in the Dutch West Indies. There, Sgt. Colvin was stricken with malaria, and began having considerable pain in a hip and leg. At the Fort Reed hospital on Trinidad, the doctors determined that a rapid weight loss had damaged his sciatic nerve. Just before Christmas 1943, he was transferred to the Halloran General Hospital on Staten Island, New York.

"On New Year's Day they put me aboard a hospital train and shipped me to Ashford, where I received a special diet and was given physical therapy. We had good care. We were four men to a room, and the doctors saw us every day. I didn't see that many nurses, but lots of ward men. One of my three roommates was a black soldier, but I don't remember anyone too well. I didn't get to know many people.

"During my three months there, I saw General Eisenhower and some other top generals. A bunch of us sitting in the hotel lobby saw 'Ike' being fitted out with the first 'Eisenhower jacket.' Colonel Beck helped him try it on. We had lots of crippled or badly burned airmen at the hospital. I remember that some were put in the swimming pool on wooden boards so they could exercise in the water."

Like Charles Colvin, a majority of Ashford patients arrived by hospital train. The typical train consisted of sixteen ward cars, each with eight double-decker bunks, and toilets and medicine cabinets; cars for staff officers, enlisted

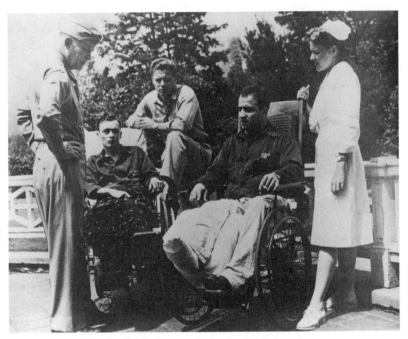

General Dwight D. Eisenhower talking with patients and a nurse on an outdoor patio (courtesy The Greenbrier).

men, and baggage; and a kitchen, dining, and pharmacy car. Trains accommodated litter cases as well as ambulatory wounded, and the Army doctors and nurses made regular "rounds." Though patients might receive candy bars, cigarettes, magazines, or newspapers from helpful Red Cross volunteers, many just wanted to sleep.

Maurice V. Mann grew up in Union, West Virginia. After his father's death, he took over the family farm and the care of his mother. Drafted in October 1942, he took basic training at Fort Riley, Kansas, then was sent to Fort Knox, Kentucky, to learn to drive tanks and half-tracks, and served overseas with the 52nd Armored Infantry Battalion, a part of the 9th Armored Division. Corporal Mann was wounded, then captured, on December 19, 1944, during the Battle of the Bulge. After four months in German prison camps, he had lost twenty-five pounds and developed serious stomach disorders:

"My last prisoner of war camp was in Bremen, Germany, where I was liberated by the British on April 28, 1945. After a month's care, I was returned to the States, arriving June

Pvt. Maurice Mann,
October 1942, before
heading overseas.

8, 1945, then was sent to Ashford, only twenty-five miles from my home. After all of the deprivation and mistreatment of the German prison camps, this was like going to heaven.

"The hospital was a wonderful place. We had good food, good treatment, and weren't crowded. But there was still shrapnel working itself out of me, and my insides were all messed up. My roomates had similar problems. It took a heck of a long time getting rested up again. After they started letting me go home on two-week leaves, the time went by pretty fast.

"I spent over six months at Ashford, receiving a certificate of disability discharge November 24, 1945. Even then, I was a long time getting well enough to do any kind of work. For a while I kept cattle, then I drove a school bus for sixteen years. I still get over to the Greenbrier sometimes — it's only thirty minutes away — and I get a great meal because a number of my neighbors work there."

Elmo Davis grew up in Ballangee, West Virginia, and worked on a farm until drafted in November 1942. A rifleman in the 85th Infantry Division, his left arm was hit and mangled by mortar fire outside Cassino, Italy, on May 12, 1944. After several days in a field hospital and some weeks in a Naples hospital, he was returned to the States. Pfc. Davis spent five weeks in other hospitals before arriving at Ashford at the end of July 1944:

"By this time, my arm was pretty well healed, except that I'd lost a piece of bone out of it. To protect my arm from possible fracture, I arrived at Ashford with a brace on it. They removed a piece of bone from my leg and put it into my arm to replace the part that had been destroyed. But first they did some skin grafts from my belly to my arm, in order to get it ready for the bone implant. This all took a long time, but time seemed to be no object there. After most of the healing was done, I spent a lot of time in a wheelchair and got very good at pushing one backwards, using just my good leg, the one they hadn't taken bone from.

Visiting day, Easter 1943 (courtesy The Greenbrier).

"I went anywhere in the hospital that I wanted to. Though I didn't do it, some of the boys would race their wheelchairs down the hill to the golf clubhouse, have a few beers, then try to walk back. They might tear their casts to pieces, but nobody'd say anything to them. They'd just fit them with new casts.

"After they put a leg iron on my cast, I walked downtown a couple of times, but that was about my limit. I went with someone who had a car down to the Pines club once or twice, and I saw a lot of USO shows (the girls were the best part). I shot some baskets in the gym, and saw the medical detachment basketball team play several games. They were great, but their games were poorly attended."

Ashford's gymnasium was a large wooden building (160' long by 100' wide) built in 1944 at a cost of $73,000. Besides the regulation-size basketball court, there were shower and locker rooms and seats for six hundred spectators; handball and boxing rooms; and exercise equipment including weights, vaulting horses, and wrestling mats. The gym also provided a heated, sheltered area for group calisthentics on cold or rainy days. Special entertainments were held there as well. A "Country Fair" held on April 27, 1945, attracted fifteen hundred revelers. Bingo, magic acts, a man who "sleeps and eats under water," a "nose reconditioning" sideshow, clowns and pitchmen, and a wheel of fortune provided something for everyone.

The Army-built gym used for physical therapy classes, dances, "country fairs," basketball games and other athletic events (courtesy The Greenbrier).

Joseph A. Giardina enlisted in the Army in 1934, completed his three-year hitch and was discharged, but re-enlisted in 1939. In September 1941, he was with the first group of B-17 bombers assigned to Clark Field in the Philippines. Two days before the Japanese sneak attack on Pearl Harbor, S/Sgt. Giardina and his 14th Bombardment Squadron was dispatched a thousand miles south to Del Monte Field on Mindanao:

"Though we flew several missions on which I served as the radio operator and top turret gunner, we soon lost most of our planes. I was captured along with others by the Japanese and taken by ship to Manila. After two nights in the Bilibad Prison, we reboarded, joined then by many of the men who had been part of the infamous Bataan Death March.

"We were big bruisers compared to them. They were all just skin and bones. We next landed at Pusan, Korea, where the men from Bataan were put on box cars and taken to Mukden to work in the mines. The rest of us went on to land at Osaka, Japan, and were sent by overnight train to Tokyo. There we were marched through the streets to a POW camp in Kawasaki, and were put to work in the steel mills.

"When I got to that camp, I still felt strong and my mind was clear. I was determined to do what I could to survive. When I was offered any kind of pill, I took it, and I ate everything they put in front of me: rice, barley, maize (pidgeon feed), some kind of watery soup, and green tea, three times a day. I survived nearly four years with no worse damage than losing seventy pounds.

"The Army got us home pretty quickly after the war. From San Francisco it took only three days by hospital train to reach White Sulphur Springs. What a beautiful place!

"They gave me a bunch of tests and chest X-rays. But I began to get scared when each day I saw my buddies leaving while I stayed behind. Finally, I asked my doctor, 'what gives?' He said they had found a suspicious scar on a lung that made it look like I might have had a problem. When he added that it seemed healed, what a load off my chest!

"At Ashford, we could eat whenever we wanted to, and they loaded us up on vitamins and all the good stuff. I started to gain weight right away. I don't remember anyone by name, because I was only there a month, but there was a nurse who used complain to the doctors a lot about a card-playing pal of mine who wouldn't stay in bed for his pills. How could he stay put with so much to see and do? Almost every night my brother would call from Brooklyn. 'When're you coming home?' he'd ask. I told him, 'Quit worrying. When I come home, I come home.'"

The "Wheelchair Brigade" on the north lawn, an Army sedan parked in the drive, hospital power plant in left background (courtesy Beulah Carpenter).

While bedridden men had bedside phones, other patients and post personnel made their calls at the "Attendant Telephone Center" in the hospital's lower level. Several young women placed hundreds of long-distance calls daily, announcing to waiting customers which booths to take. After 7:30 P.M when night rates went into effect, callers might stand shoulder-to-shoulder, and holidays were hectic.

Following V-J Day, a 45-minute musical quiz show called "The Telephone Hour" was held in a different ward every day. The men who correctly named the most song titles could win up to fifteen-minutes of free person-to-person calls. Directories for major cities were available near the Telephone Center. A huge wall map of the United States with a string anchored at White Sulphur Springs was nearby. The string was used by the men who wanted to estimate how far they were from home.

William J. O'Donnell, from Taunton, Massachusetts, was a trainee in the Army Specialized Training Program (ASTP) at Brooklyn College. When that program was cut back, he went into the 75th Infantry Division, then to the 28th Infantry Division. In late 1944, after eight days of combat in the Huertgen Forest without the protection of winter boots or galoshes, both of his feet were severely frostbitten. Private O'Donnell was evacuated, by way of Liege, Belgium, back to the 100th General Hospital in Paris:

"I was flown back to the States via the Azores and Bermuda with a cast on each foot. The trip took thirty hours, many of them spent on the ground, and I was held in the hospital at Mitchel Field for around ten days. There they only tried to keep me comfortable and watch for infection. I was flown to White Sulphur Springs on December 15, 1944, and remained there until July 7, 1945.

"My room at the hospital had a high ceiling and lots of ornate woodwork, and I'll always remember that my first meal featured fried clams. At the beginning of my stay, I had a private room, but later one with three roommates. Two of the men had frostbite and the other, Buerger's disease, which is a vascular inflammation that often leads to gangrene. We had beds with box springs, a private bath, and a carpeted floor.

"I had three operations, eventually losing all the toes on my right foot and two of the toes on my left. At first, the healing was slow because of the bone fragments working their way out. After their removal, the healing speeded up.

Pvt. William O'Donnell (far l.) and pals.

"Frostbite is a terrible thing. My case wasn't nearly as bad as one of my roommates, who had to have both feet amputated at the ankles. Another roommate, like me, just lost some toes. In spite of all this, we kidded around so much the doctors and nurses called ours the 'happy room.'

"One fellow and I rolled our wheelchairs around with our legs stuck straight out in front, and our feet bandaged in white gauze. At Christmas time, we tied red and green bows on them, and this made quite a hit. We were among the less seriously hurt patients, and were cheerful and relieved to have survived combat.

"The Salvation Army brought Christmas gifts to patients, and readers of the *Washington Times-Herald* sent presents to some patients whose names the newspaper had mentioned. Of course there were also the gifts from families and friends. We had a windowsill full of things. On New Year's Eve, a nurse gave us shot glasses of 'medicinal' whiskey so we could toast the future.

Some of the Ashford staff's many children meet Santa Claus under an icicle-draped Christmas tree (courtesy Shirley Fritchen).

"It was pretty soft living. After breakfast in the dining room, we'd sit around in the lobby listening to someone play the organ, then a little black lady would bring around a tea cart with demitasse and cookies. Every day or two a combo of Special Service musicians would come by the ward to play our requests like 'Together,' 'Always,' and 'Don't Fence Me In.' In a name-that-tune contest, I came in third, which I thought was pretty good.

"One day a roommate and I went downtown in our wheelchairs to get some lunch. That was a no-no. We passed and saluted an officer, and he must have reported us to the MPs because we'd just been served when they came in and got us. We had to leave lunch behind. The MPs got two civilians to push us up the slight hill to the hospital, and we were escorted to Colonel Beck's office where he scolded us sternly. What he didn't know was that we were sitting on cushions we'd taken from his special sofa, the one that sat up front in the War Department Theater. Those cushions fit our wheelchair seats perfectly, and covered in pillow cases, weren't noticeable.

"Several times I caught some trout in the stream that ran through the golf course. Another guy in the ward scaled them for us, and we fried them in butter in a stolen skillet on a hotplate. Of course, cooking in any of the rooms was against the rules. When an officer smelled the fish frying and came by, we thought we were in for it. Instead, he enjoyed some with us, then told us to be more discreet the next time."

Howard's Creek, home to both brown and rainbow trout, ran southwesterly through White Sulphur Springs, then past the Casino and through the golf courses. On its way to empty into the Greenbrier River it looped around the prisoner of war camp enclosure, crossing and recrossing U.S. Route 60, which it more or less paralleled. About twenty to thirty feet wide, its flow was gentle (except after thunderstorms or springtime snow melts), and it was a pleasant stream in which to fish. This same narrow stream, however, proved a dreaded hazard for golfers and a place for POW maintenance crews to find lost balls.

Clinton J. Beuscher grew up in Freeport, Illinois. He was a member of the Enlisted Reserve Corps (ERC) at North Central College in Naperville, Illinois, when called to active duty in February 1943. After basic training in the infantry, he transferred to the Army Air Forces (previously the Army Air Corps) and was sent to Kent State College in Ohio for three months as an Air Cadet. He earned his navigator's wings in September 1944, and flew to England in January 1945 as part of a replacement crew aboard a B-17 Flying Fortress:

"After my first couple of missions, my nose and cheeks began to swell, and they kept getting worse. After my twelfth, I met my brother in London. We'd seen each other a year and a half before, but with my swollen face he didn't know me. By my eighteenth, I had to hold the oxygen mask to my face with my left hand, because if I'd strapped it on in the usual way the straps would've forced my eyes closed. I badly wanted to complete the tour of thirty missions, but was grounded after flying the twenty-fourth on April 19, 1945.

"I went through three different hospitals in England before returning to the United States. I spent four months at Shick General Hospital in Clinton, Iowa, and another month at the hospital in Coral Gables, Florida, before going to Ashford. I arrived in White Sulphur Springs very early the morning of Christmas Day, 1945. I remember sitting in the train station for hours waiting for someone to take me to the hospital.

"By the time I was admitted to Ashford, my nose and cheeks were inflamed, and the swelling looked like a bad case of hives. The diagnosis was rosacea, secondary to rhinophyma. My case was considered rather rare, because rosacea seldom strikes before the age of forty, and I was only twenty-two.

"Of all the Army hospitals I came to know, Ashford was by far and away the best. In addition to the care given me by my own ward doctors, I had the benefit of consultations by visiting doctors from Walter Reed and other hospitals. My attending physician was Lieutenant Delbert V. Newcomer, who reported to the ward physician, Captain William Engstrom. I shared a room with three other fellows, one of whom had the worst case of boils I've ever seen. They were on his back, across his shoulders to the waist, and down each side. They took hours to lance, and even then they didn't heal well.

"Another guy I met, who had picked up a skin disease in the South Pacific, had a private, climate-controlled room where he spent most of his time stark naked. Another fellow, from Montana, couldn't sleep. He'd remain wide awake for three or four days before dozing off for an hour or two, and then go three or four more days wide awake.

"Being an ambulatory patient, I moved around rather freely, and played many rounds of golf. I met Sam Snead one morning in March and while he had his foursome already, meeting such a celebrity was nice. The golf courses were challenging, but well kept and fun to play. I enjoyed lots of morning coffee sessions at the clubhouse, and often played duplicate bridge in the evenings. I left the hospital in early May, and was discharged a few days later at Fort Sheridan, Illinois."

Samuel Jackson ("Sam") Snead began his long association with The Greenbrier as its golf professional in 1936. Though only twenty-three years old, his skill in hitting long drives was already legendary. After a 1942-1944 stint in the U.S. Navy, he returned to White Sulphur Springs on several occasions to play exhibition matches before crowds from the hospital, and to offer free lessons to groups of patients. Snead was again the Greenbrier "pro" from 1947 to 1974. During that time he became an international golf celebrity. In 1993, at the age of 81, he returned as The Greenbrier's "Golf Pro Emeritus."

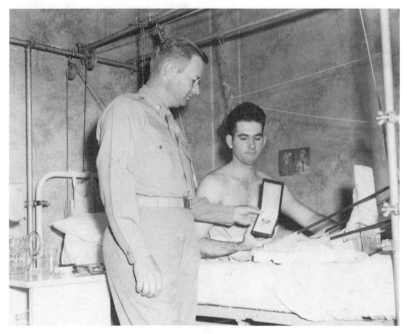

Due to long paperwork trails, many men received their Purple Hearts and awards for valor only after reaching Ashford (courtesy J.W. Benjamin, Jr.).

Kenneth E. Rinke entered active service in 1941 as an Oregon Air National Guard aerial photographer. By May 1943, when he reached North Africa, he was a first lieutenant in the Troop Carrier Command. As his squadron's adjutant and intelligence officer, he flew over many "disputed positions," experienced several minor crashes, and survived many "very, very rough" landings:

"For several months after the invasion of Sicily, I refused hospital admission for a back injury. By November, how-

ever, the flight surgeon insisted on X-raying my back and
when he saw the crushed vertebrae, that was end of my
flying. I was eventually shipped home aboard a hospital
ship, and arrived at Ashford by train in May 1944. I was
there three or four weeks while they took more X-rays and
did more tests. The doctors found several herniated disks,
and others that were severely inflamed. They discussed
putting me in a body cast, but concluded that could wait
and I was then transferred to Baxter General Hospital in
Spokane, Washington, nearer home.

Capt. Kenneth E.
Rinke and his wife,
Sybil, enjoy spring
sunshine, 1945.

"My roommate at Ashford was a guy named Art Sykes.
We'd met and become friends back in Casablanca, and
had returned home on the same hospital ship. Our wives
actually reached White Sulphur Springs the same day we

did. They found and shared an apartment in town and became close friends, too. One day the four of us were walking around the grounds, when I heard some German POWs talking. Being captives and away from women so long they were naturally discussing the two pretty girls. I knew some German, so I walked over and said, 'macht nichts aus,' or something like that, meaning 'cut it out.' Judging from their startled looks you might have thought they feared being shot or hung for their indiscretion. Actually they had my sympathy rather than animosity. Anyway, from then on they gave us plenty of respect. They might ignore other officers but for us they'd click their heels sharply.

"I'd heard of the Greenbrier before being sent there. I knew it was famous for its golf courses and that it had been used for the internment of Axis diplomats. Since I had to wear a back brace, and Art used crutches, we didn't do many things. Occasionally, just to escape the hospital ambience for a few hours, we'd eat out with our wives at a downtown restaurant. We liked Ashford, and even under the circumstances, enjoyed our stay there."

Apart from obvious limitations on their freedom, the German prisoners at Ashford lived relatively pleasant lives. They were well clothed and fed, and had permission to make their barracks as homelike as possible. Each company of a hundred men was allowed one radio, which could be listened to every evening after work (though almost to the end of the war, all broadcasts suggesting that Germany was losing were dismissed as propaganda). Many of these soldiers — none were officers — had won medals for bravery. They remained proud men, and wore their "PW" emblazoned uniforms with some dignity. They were treated well — completely in accord with the Geneva Convention.

Arthur Sykes had almost finished college when the Japanese attacked Pearl Harbor. A year and a half later, he led an infantry platoon in the invasion of Sicily. Later, during the campaign up the Italian mainland, he was badly wounded in both his back and right knee by German artillery and mortar fire. By the time First Lt. Sykes arrived at Ashford, he was well enough to get around on crutches:

"After Ken Rinke and I met, we enjoyed each other's company a lot. The fact that we both played bridge so well drew us together. We organized our own tournaments, and played as a team for small stakes.

First Lt. Arthur Sykes and his wife, Jean, in that same wonderful spring of 1945.

"Ashford was a fine hospital and they took great care of us. In addition to my numerous shrapnel wounds, I'd developed a brain tumor as a result of all the concussions I'd suffered. They had to remove the tumor, and it was quite an operation. I was a long time recuperating, and I'm still a bit limited. My coordination is very poor, and I won't win any footraces, but I can live with it."

While bridge was a popular activity at the Officer's Club, many bridge enthusiasts took part in tournaments arranged by Red Cross Recreation Director Irene Spitz. Known throughout the hospital as "The Human Dynamo," the indefatigable Spitz, like her staff of some twenty office and social workers, was a paid fulltime Red Cross employee. Dozens of Gray Ladies, Nurse's Aides, and other part-time Red Cross volunteers gave countless hours in support of the paid staff.

It was a Gray Lady who changed forever the life of Ashford patient Ralph Fisk. Inducted in November 1942, Fisk served with the 39th Combat Engineers and took part in landings in North Africa, Sicily, and Italy. Corporal Fisk was hit in the legs and hip by German artillery as he slept. A man in the next tent was killed outright by the same shell:

"If my head had been where my feet were, I wouldn't be here today. I'd been asleep, with my head on my arm, and woke up thinking I had a 'charlie horse' in my leg. I reached down and found blood all over me. They got me to battalion aid, where they dusted me with sulpha powder then gave me a shot of something to kill the pain. I'll swear it was only water. Then they put me in an ambulance to take me back to a field hospital. I thought I was going to die from all the jolting.

"At the field hospital, they took me into the operating room and covered my face with a mask. I thought, 'Thank God, now the pain will stop.' I didn't know if I'd ever come to, or what would happen, but I knew I was out of the war. Sometime during the night I woke up and a nurse was sitting beside my bed. I asked her if my leg had been amputated and she said it hadn't. I went back to sleep, but soon woke up and asked the same question. Again the nurse said, 'No,' and then asked if I wanted to see my toes. By this time I was in a body cast with an iron bar spacing my legs apart. The cast had cut-outs for my toes, and when I saw them sticking out I knew she was telling the truth.

Cpl. Ralph Fisk (l.) and friend in Sicily, August 1943.

"A few weeks later they took me to the general hospital in Florence. I was getting ready to enjoy a good Thanksgiving dinner, when the doctors came by asking how I was. I said I had kernel-like swollen places all over me. When they asked where, and I said in my arm pits and groin, they said, 'Uh, oh,' and put me down for immediate surgery to take out what proved to be a blood clot. I was given a local anesthetic, and I didn't even miss dinner. Two weeks later I was sent home. I remember distinctly that they never gave me enough painkiller. They said it might make me a drug addict.

"Our hospital train pulled into the White Sulphur Springs station about 2 A.M. At that time, I had never heard of the Greenbrier, hardly even of West Virginia. When we stopped, I thought we were in some cow pasture. I had expected to see a lot of city lights, but there weren't any. They took me out through a window because I was still a litter case, and took me by ambulance to the hospital, only five minutes away.

"At Ashford, I had twenty operations, spending much of the time there in a very hot and uncomfortable cast and with a bad burning feeling in my ankle. I finally got used to it, and I did get plenty of painkillers.

"When I finally started getting better, one of my doctors asked me, 'Son, how long's it been since you've been home?' When I said it'd been over two years he told me that all I had to do was get up on crutches. The first time I put my legs on the floor, I thought they'd burst, and when I went to therapy for my first whirlpool bath, I didn't expect to make it. But I was only twenty-five, and in pretty good shape, so I did a lot of hopping. (I was able to go home four times in all, but, because my mother had died in 1943, home was never the same.)

"At Ashford, the Gray Ladies were just great. They'd come to your room and read to you, and fetch you things, and do everything they could to make you comfortable. One day my favorite, a Mrs. Kyle Erwin, brought her daughter, Ann. We hadn't met, and didn't know anything about each other, but it was love at first sight for both of us. From then on, there were a lot of Sunday dinners with the Erwins. Ann's father, Kyle, would drive up from Ronceverte after church and take three or four of us guys home with him.

"On other days, Ann would come up to the hospital and push me around the grounds in my wheelchair. On one especially sunny day, Colonel Beck stopped and warned me, 'Young man, you'd better get back indoors. You're turning pretty pink.' We followed his suggestion promptly.

Ann Erwin (center) and friends "making like the Andrew Sisters" for an Ashford entertainment (courtesy Ralph Fisk).

"For a time there at Ashford, all of us fellows looked like pincushions, with the nurses coming hourly to give someone a shot. I've been told we were among the first patients to get penicillin in massive doses. I liked to sit in my wheelchair down in the lobby and drink coffee and munch cookies from a tea cart they pushed around. I also enjoyed listening to the Moeller pipe organ, a grand instrument with three keyboards.

"In fact, there's a very good story about that organ. After the war, when the hospital became a resort hotel again, the owners decided they didn't need it — this was in late 1946 after Ann and I had been married and settled in Ronceverte. When the minister of our Presbyterian Church found out that private bids on the organ would be considered, he approached the property manager saying that he wasn't authorized by the church to go higher than $500. To everyone's amazement, this offer was accepted. The church then spent another $3,500 to have the organ installed. Ann now plays it every Sunday and today it's worth more than $200,000."

George D. Kennedy, from Rivesville, West Virginia, was drafted in 1943, wounded in Italy, then wounded again, more seriously, on October 7, 1944, in France. Private Kennedy was an infantryman in the 36th Infantry Division:

"We came back from Europe on an ordinary transport, not a hospital ship, with wounded like me placed in the various officers' cabins. When we entered New York harbor, I just had to go topside to see the Statue of Liberty and the tall buildings, so, dressed in my pajamas and field jacket, I got a friend to help me to hop up the steps. An officer spotted us, and gave me hell for risking my good leg on an icy deck. They kept me at Halloran General Hospital for a week or so, then asked where I'd like to go. I said 'West Virginia,' of course.

"On the train ride that followed, several men were dropped off at the Newton D. Baker General Hospital in Martinsburg, West Virginia, but I wasn't one of them. Further along, we went through Clarksburg, West Virginia. I felt heartbroken because I could almost see my house from the train. Don't ask why, but I ended up in the Harmon General Hospital in Longview, Texas.

"In December, while at home on convalescent leave, I got pneumonia. My family doctor arranged that I be admitted to the nearest military hospital, which happened to be Ashford, and my father and mother rushed me to White Sulphur Springs. A local mechanic converted the part of the front seat on the passenger's side so that it laid back almost like a bed. My wife went along in the back seat and comforted me during the trip.

"I was bedridden at first, and I had a couple of roommates. My wife had a room in town while I was there, and she came to see me every day from two until four each afternoon and again from six until eight every evening. When an orderly asked what she did between visits, she told him she either bought dinner in the cafeteria or downtown. He got really angry. 'If the Army can afford to feed the German POWs so good,' he said, 'it sure as hell can feed a wounded G.I.'s wife.' After that, she had dinners with me in my room.

"When I'd recovered from pneumonia, instead of sending me back to Texas, they kept me at Ashford to remove some more shrapnel from my legs. Soon I was able to get around in a wheelchair, and my wife pushed me different places, like to the barbershop. After the doctors had removed all the shrapnel they could, they told me 'just go home and rest but don't work for a while.' I went home June 15, 1945."

Carlos H. Walls, Jr. suffered a severe head injury while in training with the 104th Mountain Infantry near Seneca Rocks, West Virginia. He remained unconscious for thirty days and was not expected to live. During three months at Ashford he gradually regained his strength but his wife Nancy says "he had to learn to walk and talk again, just like a baby." She remembers her visits to the hospital:

"I was working for a coal company in McDowell County at the time, but on weekends I'd go up to White Sulphur

Springs by bus. That meant going to Bluefield on a Friday evening and staying in a hotel, then catching the first bus I could the next morning. The bus stopped right at the hospital's gate. I always returned home the same day.

Carlos and Nancy Walls kiss during a stroll past the famous Springhouse. She visited her husband as often as possible, riding the bus between Bluefield and White Sulphur Springs, a long trip each way .

"When Carlos was strong enough, we'd walk around the grounds and talk about the future. Someone once took a photograph of us embracing near the Springhouse. Carlos never completely recovered physically, but we are both still very involved in veterans' affairs, particularly with the West Virginia VFW."

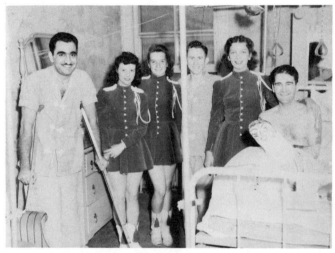

Drum majorettes from Charleston's Stonewall Jackson High School visited bedridden patients who missed their outdoor baton-twirling show (courtesy Ralph Fisk).

A favorite destination for strolling patients and visitors was the famous old Springhouse. Dating back to the early 1830s, it always has been the physical and symbolic center of the resort, and an ideal place to pose for photographs. The first statue atop the Springhouse was that of *Hygeia*, goddess of health. After the statue disappeared during the Civil War, a substitute was installed in the mid-1870s. The substitute statue was of *Hebe,* goddess of youth, and it was she that Ashford patients and visitors saw while passing by the Springhouse. Though anyone could draw and drink a glass of the water, the sulphurous odor may have deterred all but the most determined. The hospital's drinking, cooking, and bathing water came from a mountain spring miles away.

Ben Wechsler was born in Pittsburgh, Pennsylvania, and had earned an engineering degree at Carnegie Tech before going into the Army. He was with the 307th Airborne Engineers when the unit parachuted into Sicily in July 1943. During a fight against German tanks he was wounded in the right leg by machine gun fire. Though pulled to temporary safety by some of his men, he lay untended for two days, then spent three months in a hospital in Oujda, Morocco, before coming home by ship:

"At Oujda, the doctors at first believed my right leg might have to be amputated. Two inches of bone had been shot away and they feared I might have gangrene. When it proved I did not, they put me into traction. They drilled horizontally through the tibia just below the break and inserted a steel pin so that it stuck out both sides of my leg. My leg then was suspended and weights hung from each of the pins. This traction kept the bones the right distance apart while they mended. Also, they fed me lots of calcium to help form new bone tissue. When I was well enough to take home, I was put into a body cast that came up above my waist. I was still in the cast when I got to Ashford General around the middle of November 1943.

"They didn't really do any more medically for me at Ashford. They just removed the cast and let me convalesce. To help pass the time, several of us organized special study classes on subjects that we could either teach, or in which we could learn something new. That was very satisfying.

"One of the very sad things I remember from my months at Ashford was a local man whose son had been reported missing in action with my division, the 82nd Airborne. He had been coming to the hospital regularly to try to find someone who knew of his son. One day, he talked to me and it turned out the young man had been in my platoon. The man insisted that I tell him what had happened. Though I truly didn't know, I suspected that his son had been killed — very terribly — in the same action in which I'd been wounded. Some of the German tanks churning through the vineyards where we fought ground some of our men to pieces. I couldn't tell the man that, even if I'd known it to be true.

"One of my ward nurses was a Lieutenant Smith, at least I think that was her name. Everyone just called her 'Smitty.' She lived in one of the cottages, Tansas A, with several of the other nurses, and that's how I met Bonnie, my wife-to-be. She had grown up in Columbus, Ohio, and, like Smitty, was an Army nurse.

"Soon I was up and around on crutches and leg braces, and I began courting Bonnie pretty seriously. We went out in the evenings for dinners at the Eagle's Nest and the Pines. If I gave them enough advance notice, the Eagle's Nest would find some steak and we'd have a steak and champagne dinner. There was also the Chicken Shack, a black-owned spot that made the best southern fried chicken you ever ate. Also, we attended some affairs at the Officer's Club, and enjoyed the swimming pool a lot.

"When we decided to get married, Bonnie's supervisors didn't like the idea and tried to talk her out of it. Somebody even initiated paperwork to move her overseas. But we went ahead and were married in the hospital chapel on May 27, 1944. The post chaplain, Robert H. Clarke, performed the ceremony, and Colonel Beck gave the bride away. We held a small reception in one of the cottages.

"I'd been discharged from the hospital in April, and had returned for the wedding ceremony from Camp Sutton, North Carolina. Though Bonnie didn't receive any time off for the wedding, they gave her a week's honeymoon leave. After that I went back to Camp Sutton, and in a short while Bonnie was shipped overseas to Europe. When she proved to be pregnant, she was sent home and discharged.

"I stayed in the service, and after having had tours of duty in Korea and the Pentagon and having taught military science at Lehigh University, retired as a Colonel. Bonnie and I had a good life, and raised three daughters and two sons. Before she died in 1993, we had returned to the Greenbrier several times, once for our 35th anniversary. We took two cottages, and all our children and grandchildren were with us. Since that's where I first met Bonnie, it was an extremely happy time. It all began at Ashford General."

Marriages between Ashford nurses and patients, although not rare, were somewhat infrequent. The Army tried to head off disruptive resignations by "protecting" its nurses from any and all romantic entanglements. More common were weddings involving resident patients and their girl friends from back home, or those between medical detachment men and hospital civil service employees.

Dana J. Keaton, from the Hinton, West Virginia area, was drafted in March 1944, and became a U.S. Navy gunner aboard a merchant ship in a North Atlantic convoy. After returning from his first crossing, he was going home on leave when his appendix burst. Since any serviceman with an urgent medical problem could seek help at the nearest military hospital, he was rushed to Ashford:

"I was in the hospital five weeks. An infection set in just about the time I'd normally have been released. They said I was the only sailor there, just me and some eighteen hundred soldiers. They razzed me a bit, but it was all in good fun. I was impressed by the fine treatment I received, especially from a young Red Cross Nurse's Aide. I was only eighteen and trying to grow a moustache to seem older. Every day she'd darken that fuzz with some mascara to help it show up more. Ashford was really neat."

Dana J. Keaton in boot camp. He was one of the few sailors treated at Ashford.

Charles E. Merritt was another sailor who was treated at Ashford. As a seventeen-year-old Pharmacist's Mate 2nd Class, he had been one of the four hundred men in the U.S. Navy 7th Beach Battalion that laid out Omaha Beach landing zones on D-Day 1944:

"It was hard to tell us from the Army, but we were Navy all the way. Our job was to place the beach markers that showed where the infantry was supposed to land. We were in landing craft manned by attack transport personnel before daybreak, and on the beach itself just after dawn. Many were killed. A bomb concussion messed up my leg, but I could limp around okay and I didn't want to come off the beach.

"I remained there nearly a month. During that time, I saw the engineers make an artificial harbor by lining up rows of freighters, bow to stern, then scuttling them in the shallow water just off shore. I particularly remember one very badly wounded soldier who'd stepped on a land mine. Though it all happened almost fifty years ago, he's written twice to thank me for saving his life. He lost both legs below the knee but he says he's fine, and still goes dancing.

"Anyway, I had returned to the U.S. and was on leave at my home near Beckley, West Virginia, when my knee began to act up. My father made the arrangements, and an Army ambulance came and took me up to White Sulphur Springs. That was just great. I had always wanted to see the inside of the famous Greenbrier, and this was my chance.

"Well, they X-rayed my knee, and then put a cast on it. They said the ligaments and cartilages were all torn up, and that I'd need an operation, but in the end, all they did was give me physical therapy plus a wheelchair and crutches.

"We were four or five men to a room, and pretty crowded. But I was well cared for, and very very happy to be so close to home that my father and my sister (my mother was dead) could drive up to visit me. I saw some movies, but none of the USO shows or the big name stars. They kept me about thirty-five days, then sent me on to the naval hospital at Camp LeJeune, North Carolina."

Going to the movies in the hospital theater was a favorite diversion for many patients. The films usually changed five times a week. Those with pretty girls were predictably the most popular. In one banner week, the men could watch, one after another, "Andy Hardy's Blonde Trouble," starring June Pressier; "Her Primitive Man," with Louise Albritton; "Moon Over Las Vegas," with Anne Gwynne; and "Pin-Up Girl," with the G.I.'s all-time favorite, Betty Grable.

Ken Jackson, from Huntington, West Virginia, enlisted at age eighteen. He flew fourteen missions as a S/Sgt. tailgunner in B-17s based at Foggia, Italy. Just after V-J Day, he was home on leave when he developed pneumonia. He was taken to Ashford by ambulance, and remained four weeks:

"Ashford was winding down when I was there, and the general atmosphere was really relaxed. I recall Sunday 'tea dances' where some of the guys wore 'zoot suits' made from cut-down Army jackets — not the short 'Ike' jackets, but the other, longer ones. My stay coincided with the arrival of lots of Bataan Death March survivors. I didn't see him, but I think General Jonathan Wainwright wrote his memoirs at Ashford.*

"I didn't go out much, because I didn't feel so hot. One of my roommates, a former P-47 fighter pilot, had a car and we drove to Lewisburg once to see a Greenbrier Military

---

* Wainwright's war diary notes, that with help from sports writer Bob Considine, he began "My Story" for the International News Service at Ashford's "Top Notch Cottage" on September 20, 1945. Coincidentally, General John J. Pershing, famed hero of the First World War, had once completed his memoirs in the same cottage.

School football game. Ashford patients were admitted free, and we enjoyed watching the boys bang each other around."

Staff Sgt. Ken Jackson, tailgunner, beside his B-17 Flying Fortress while still in training in Florida. Treated for pneumonia, he was later found to have had mononucleosis.

The Greenbrier Military School, closed since 1972, was the oldest privately operated military school in the country. Its students excelled not only scholastically but in sports as well. At least one of its alumni was an Ashford patient: Cpl. Arthur McPherson, who was wounded in Italy, was quoted in an Associated Press story as saying, "When I used to come over with the cadets from the military school to swim in the pool here, I didn't visualize the day when I would be taking swimming as [physical therapy] treatment."

Warren G. Cox of Richwood, West Virginia, was an ASTPer at Rhode Island State College before his transfer to the Sixth Armored Division at Nancy, France, in October 1944. He was wounded near Bastogne, Belgium, in the

Battle of the Bulge, and hospitalized overseas until May 1945. Pfc. Cox returned to the U.S. at the end of that month:

"At first I was sent to a hospital in Texas, apparently by mistake. Then in June, I was sent back east, fortunately to Ashford General Hospital, just seventy miles from home. I'd been ambulatory since March, and was nearly fully recovered from a shrapnel wound in the chest. I was given a weekend leave and my parents came to pick me up.

Warren Cox and his wife, Ella, at a college picnic in 1946. Ella was expecting their first child, Shari.

"The rest of my time at Ashford was spent waiting for the chest cavity to heal from the inside out. That took until the end of November. I was at home much of the time, just returning to the hospital two or three times a week to have my dressings changed. I did lots of breathing exercises and physical therapy.

"One incident I remember involved General Eisenhower, who visited Ashford several times. One of the exercises I did to restore my lung strength was to blow water out of one bottle into another through various rubber tubes and stoppers. One day while I was doing this, Eisenhower came into my room and sat down on a bed. He seemed interested in me and asked lots of questions about the bottles of blue water. The treatment must have impressed him, because weeks later, he returned to my room, and because the paraphernalia was out of sight, the very first thing he asked me was, 'Where are your bottles?'

"I also played lots of golf on the Greenbrier and Old White courses. That was great for a poor boy who had caddied on a little nine hole course with sand 'greens' in Richwood. I'd learned to play with only a few clubs, and had saved enough money, perhaps around six dollars, to buy a brassie, a five iron, and a putter from Montgomery Ward.

"Ashford was unlike any other military post I'd ever seen. When I got there I was told we could wear any clothes within reason, either military or civilian. We weren't required to salute officers or pull any duty. We could go for meals any time within a two-hour period and the tables had white linen tablecloths and napkins. Holiday dinners were super. At Thanksgiving there was a cornucopia of fruit in the lobby outside the dining room that I could hardly believe.

"On one of my leaves from the hospital, I married my high school sweetheart, Ella Vesta Fitzwater. Like lots of other couples, we eloped to Ashland, Kentucky. After that, I was given a succession of convalescent leaves, and spent little time at Ashford. I hitchhiked, caught a bus, or borrowed my dad's 1939 Plymouth when its tires weren't flat. My wound finally healed, and I left the Army on December 15, 1945."

At Ashford, convalescent leaves were considered essential to speeding the recovery of the patients. Colonel Beck's policy on leaves was simple:

> We try to send a patient on leave or furlough when it doesn't interfere with his treatment or prolong his period of hospitalization. There's no reason why a man who has been in combat overseas and who returns for hospitalization cannot have a furlough when he has reached the period of treatment that daily care is not required and at the same time he cannot be returned to duty.

Sitting around on a stone bench waiting to go home could be thoroughly boring (courtesy Ralph Fisk).

Carl E. Edwards, from Nimitz, West Virginia, served in the weapons platoon of Company C, 422nd Regiment, 106th Infantry Division. The last U.S. division to go overseas, the "green" 106th was surrounded by the Germans during the Battle of the Bulge, and Sgt. Edwards was captured. Taken away in railroad boxcars, he and hundreds of fellow captives were bombed and strafed by Allied aircraft, and many were killed or wounded. Moved repeatedly from camp to camp, he and his comrades were finally liberated on April 12, 1945:

"I'd lost sixty-five pounds. They flew me to Le Havre, where a doctor said that I should be hospitalized immediately, but I was so eager to get home I asked him to let me go, and he did. When I arrived at Fort Meade, Maryland, another doctor asked more questions, then gave me a sixty-day furlough. I didn't tell him, or anyone, that I'd frozen both feet while in Germany. After about a week at home, I started running a high fever. A local doctor looked at me, and said that I'd better get to a hospital fast, or I might lose both my feet. Ashford was only thirty-five miles away and I checked in on June 4, 1945.

"I was put into a room on the third floor with a fellow from Idaho and some guy from New York. My doctor was a tall, thin lieutenant colonel who was pleasant but remained remote, the way some doctors do. My feet were so badly infected they had to give me penicillin shots every three hours. I needed two months of bed rest to heal and to regain my strength.

"My parents came to visit me several times, and I actually bumped into a fellow I'd grown up with. He'd been a German prisoner, too, and his broken leg hadn't been set right, so the doctors at Ashford had to rebreak and reset it. When my feet had mostly healed, they sent me to an Army hospital in Pennsylvania, from which I was discharged November 8, 1945. Thank God I still have both my feet."

Although antibacterials such as penicillin and the so-called sulpha drugs (sulfanilamide and its many derivatives such as sulfadiazine and sulfathiazol) have been used for only fifty years or so, many call them the greatest therapeutic advance in the history of medicine. Until these drugs were available many patients routinely died of common bacterial infections.

Ashford was among the first of the Army hospitals authorized to use penicillin. Though in 1942 there was barely enough to treat a hundred patients, by late 1943 the United States was producing sufficient amounts for the armed services of every allied nation and by 1945 enough for U.S. civilians as well. Penicillin ranked beside blood plasma and frozen whole blood as the war's most effective life saver.

Aerial View, Ashford General Hospital

Patients used free postcards given to them by the American Red Cross. A printed message on the reverse read "I am now a patient at this hospital, which was formerly the famous Greenbrier Hotel."

Harold Braun, from New Jersey, entered military service in February 1941, earned a commission in July 1942, and won the Silver Star during fighting with the 158th Infantry Regiment (the famous "Bushmasters") in the Philippines. Captain Braun was wounded a second time on January 24, 1945, and his was a long journey home:

"From Luzon, the trip began aboard an LST to Leyte; then a hospital ship (the *Maetsuycker*) to Hollandia, New Guinea; a troopship (the *USS Monterey*) to San Francisco; and finally, a hospital train to White Sulphur Springs. Our March 1945 arrival had a comic touch. At Cincinnati, where we made an unscheduled stop due to mechanical problems, many of us put on our uniforms and headed into town. Though MPs eventually rounded everyone up, many in casts and heavy bandages, some men brought back concealed bottles and we all commenced celebrating our homecoming en route.

"At White Sulphur Springs, a contingent of 'big brass' was waiting for us. By then, somewhat drunk, many of the walking wounded could no longer walk, and additional wheelchairs had to be found. The 'big brass' were not amused.

"I was certainly happy to be at Ashford, a complete and total change from the jungles of the Pacific. It was like living in a dream. Seeming pretty much as it had been in peace time, the place now had a different clientele — all military — and every one of us aching to get home. While we waited, we enjoyed things we hadn't had for a long time. I recall drinking so many chocolate milkshakes the cast on my arm got tight.

"Part of Ashford's appeal was not having to do things 'by the numbers.' When I returned from home leave, I brought my 1940 Pontiac convertible. Springtime was beautiful and I was determined to get some of the more seriously wounded out and about to see it. I even dropped the top to accommodate some standees. Our very visible casts and bandages seemed to add to the hospitality we enjoyed while driving around.

"I rented a room in White Sulphur Springs for my wife,

and repapered, painted, and polished up everything to her high standards. Ashford was not always the staid old hospital a lot of people would have you think. I remember that several nurses threw a big party in one of the cottages. Liquor was purchased at the 'state store' in town, and everything was great until a fight broke out, and someone went for the MPs. That started a mad scramble, with everyone grabbing bottles and heading for the door. Everything was quiet when the MPs got there, but from then on, parties were banned.

Pvt. Hal Braun as a "damyankee" at Fort Benning, Georgia, 1941. Four years later he brought his 1940 convertible to Ashford and gave some of his friends joyrides around the countryside.

"At the hospital, people helped one another. We were the generation that had survived the Great Depression, that had won World War II, and that still had certain values. We were brought up respecting our elders. We stood when a lady came into a room. Courtesy was something we practiced, not just a word under 'C' in the dictionary.

"It was curious, too, how some of us began to feel luckier and luckier after seeing other patients in much worse shape than ourselves. I can still see one man whose lower jaw had been shot away. Using one of his own ribs, the doctors made a new jaw for him, and he communicated by writing notes. One fellow had a skin graft he called 'the drum,' because it was stretched so tight that he could tap tunes on it. Once I saw a former college football player racing down the hall in his wheelchair with a case of soda-pop on his lap. I offered to carry it because I thought it might be too heavy for him. He just said, 'It's okay. Something like that can't hurt me anymore. I'm paralyzed from the waist down.' There were many courageous people in that hospital."

The courage shown by the wounded men Harold Braun knew, and by Braun himself, was typical. Such courage was quiet and concentrated, self-deprecatingly determined not to draw attention to itself. Various postwar movies, such as "The Men," with Marlon Brando, or "The Best Years of Our Lives," with Fredric March, often portrayed war veterans as tense and aggressive, and given to violent rages. More commonly the face of courage was the quiet one seen at Ashford.

Henry P. Lawhorn, from Lynchburg, Virginia was eighteen when he enlisted in the Army in January 1942. He had three months of training near Seneca Rocks, West Virginia, where soldiers were taught mountain climbing. He went overseas in July 1944 with the 188th Combat Engineers as a demolition expert. Two months later, he was almost fatally wounded by the explosion of a land mine he and a buddy were disarming. His companion was killed while Sgt. Lawhorn lay paralyzed with head, back, and leg injuries.

He was taken to a nearby monastery by some French farmers, and from there to an Army hospital:

"They had to cut my clothes off, my shoes were gone, and I was blind. They put me on a plane to England, and later I returned to the U.S. on the *Queen Mary*.

"Heading south from New York on the train, we had a long layover in Washington, where I heard a group come aboard my car and walk down the aisle talking to everyone. I couldn't see who it was, but a man patted me very gently on the head and said, 'It's all right, son, you're home now. We'll take care of you.' Later, I was told it was President Roosevelt.

"My mother had received a telegram that told her I was dead. Because I had such extensive wounds, including a big hole in my head, nobody expected I'd live. Neither my mother nor my wife knew I was alive until I reached Woodrow Wilson General Hospital in Staunton, Virginia. I was reluctant to have them see me, because I'd lost all my hair and my face was scarred very badly. The very day my mother finally was able to come and visit me, I was moved to Ashford and missed her.

"At Woodrow Wilson General, they found a blood clot in my brain, and I was taken by Army ambulance to Ashford for an immediate operation. Later I had several more. I think the Ashford doctors were absolutely the best. They saved me. I'd heard someone on the C-54 bringing me home from Europe say I'd probably never recover because my back was broken, and I had extensive brain damage. Though I went home in a wheelchair, at least I went home!

"We got just about anything we wanted at Ashford. The food was great, and it seemed like everyone in the entertainment world came through there at one time or another. One of my roommates could play piano, so two of them grabbed one from the lounge and brought it to the room. It was just a little thing with wheels on it. We hid it in the 'john' between our room and the one next door, moving it back and forth to hide it from our nurse.

Pvt. Henry Lawhorn after having just finished special training near Seneca Rocks, West Virginia.

"Sadly, our piano player died after an operation. Many lives were saved there at Ashford, but many were lost too. From my window, I could see the C&O train station, and I watched the caskets from the hospital being loaded on the trains.

"If it hadn't been for Ashford and its skilled surgeons, a lot of us wouldn't be here today. Just think, in cases like mine, they had to pick foreign bodies from the brain, and in some cases they couldn't even get it all. It wasn't the big famous people who were patients but mostly these little buck privates fighting for life. I'm only sorry that in my pain, and my youth, I never got the names and addresses of the men and women who were so good to me and helped me live. I thank all those good Americans who cared so much."

Ashford General Hospital compiled an outstanding record. In its entire existence, there were but twenty-six deaths from operation-related causes, plus another fifty-five from such diseases such as as tuberculosis, lung cancer, and leukemia. About half the patients treated at Ashford were returned to active duty, 20 percent received a certificate of disability discharge, 10 percent were discharged for other reasons, and the remainder were patients transferred to other hospitals, or officers who retired once the war was over.

3

Doctors, Dentists, and MAC Officers

On December 7, 1941, there were about 132,000 doctors, dentists, nurses, and other officers and enlisted men in the U.S. Army Medical Department. Four years later, there were five times that many: 700,000 men and women — not counting chaplains, engineers, members of the Women's Army Corps (WAC), and various personnel from other branches who worked for the Department.

Recruiting so many health professionals, then training them in military medicine, called for an unprecedented effort. Although the Medical Department was beset by fluctuating strength-ceilings, problems of procurement, questions about the most effective use of the personnel it was assigned, awkward chains of command, and competition with other branches for support personnel (the help of 150,000 civilians, 80,000 prisoners of war, and 20,000 WACs was required) it performed magnificiently.

All of the major "officer components" of the Department were represented at Ashford General Hospital: doctors, dentists, nurses, medical administrative officers (non-doctors who did most of the hospital paperwork), veterinarians, pharmacists, physical therapists, and dieticians. Perhaps as many as 800 Medical Department officers and 1,500 enlisted men served at Ashford at one time or another.

The Casino Cottage was Colonel Clyde Beck's home. There he entertained such visitors as Gen. Jonathan Wainwright (courtesy Beulah Carpenter).

Considering the tremendous contributions of the hospital's commanding officer, Colonel Clyde M. Beck, it is appropriate to begin this chapter with the remembrances of his daughter, Eleanor Beck Kerkam, who, with her children, seven-year-old Donna and three-year-old Johnny, shared the spacious home assigned to her parents. Her husband, Capt. John Kerkam, served at Wright Field, in Dayton, Ohio, but was unable to find family housing there, and traveled by train to visit his family on weekends and holidays. Mrs. Kerkam says:

"You've probably heard a lot of good stories about father, and they're all true. He was the most wonderful man that anybody could ever imagine. He never shut the door of his office. He said, 'No, I want it open so that anybody who wants to see me can walk right in any time.' All the same, he was strict. He never let anyone get away with something they shouldn't have done.

"Father and mother knew General and Mrs. Eisenhower quite well, because father and the general had served together at the Presidio before the war, My parents became even better friends with them when the Eisenhowers came

Colonel Clyde Beck and his Doberman pinscher, "Red," with some of the famous Greenbrier cottages in the background (courtesy The Greenbrier).

to the hospital several times. When 'Ike' was elected president, my father and mother dined at the White House, and each time President Eisenhower went through Memphis (my parents' home, and where they retired), he had his presidential rail car placed on a siding for a quiet get-together with them.

"At Ashford, I contributed by serving as a nurse's aide, and I think I was probably the only girl to give shampoos to the boys strung up in traction. They were so grateful. I worked in the recovery room, too. I didn't get any training, I just did it. Mother was a Gray Lady, so you could say we all did our part.

"Donna went to school in White Sulphur Springs, but Johnny wasn't even in kindergarten yet. We had a black nanny for him but every chance he had, he'd run away to the hospital. Sometimes he'd play hide-and-seek in the theater, with the soldiers helping him to escape his nanny. He went down to the main gate one day, and of course the guard knew who he was and asked him if he wasn't Colonel Beck's little grandson. Johnny said, 'Oh no! That's another bad boy who runs away all the time.' Johnny was very precious — the best boy in the world — and he's still the love of my life.

"I very much enjoyed myself at Ashford. It really was like 'Shangri-La.' You couldn't ask for a nicer place. I played golf almost every day, as did my father. The former hotel's owners should have loved him for how well he had the courses cared for. All those redbud trees — he purchased a hundred of them with his own money. He loved the hotel and cared for all the historical parts of it. He should be commemorated in some suitable way!

"Father had an older friend who lived in Lewisburg, a Dr. Gory Hogg, and the two of them played golf regularly. They'd play even in the snow, using red balls. After his retirement my father returned to West Virginia each year to stay at his friend's home in Lewisburg, and to play golf with him in the Virginia Seniors tournament at The Greenbrier. Dr. Hogg had been the C&O doctor, and was a beautiful old gentleman from a famous Texas family. He had settled near the Greenbrier when the C&O owned it.

"My father died of cancer in 1963. Dr. Hogg's daughter called me later to tell me that when the doctor had heard of my father's death, he kind of gave up, and he died two weeks later."

General Beck's bust was cast at Ashford by soldier-sculptor Cpl. Archimedes Giacomantonio. This photo was used on a postcard that could be bought in the hospital PX (courtesy Mary Ellen Sparks Given).

The silver stars of a Brigadier General were pinned on Clyde Beck's shoulders on September 27, 1945, in a formal ceremony on the hospital's grounds. For his untiring work, Gen. Beck was given the Legion of Merit on April 13, 1946.

One of the first doctors to arrive at the hospital was Lewis T. Corum, who grew up in Corbin, Kentucky, earned his M.D. degree from the University of Tennessee in Memphis and had just completed his residency when he joined the Medical Corps. The day after he finished his indoctrination course at La Garde General Hospital in New Orleans he was assigned to report to Ashford. He took a train home, picked up his car, and drove to White Sulphur Springs, arriving two days late. Dr. Corum laughs about the first entry in his military service record that said he was two days late, but that his AWOL was excused:

"My speciality was pediatrics, which, in the Army, put me into the contagious or communicable diseases section. The hospital had just opened when I got there in November 1942, and our first patients were men from the medical detachment. They weren't yet busy, and they'd go out at night for a few beers, fool around in that raw winter climate, then come in with some respiratory problem a few days later. Plus, you had all those country boys together in barracks, where they could easily pick up some bug. They weren't used to being around so many people and hadn't built up the immunities of the city boys.

"At twenty-seven, I was one of the 'babies' on the medical staff. Though I had no skills in military protocol, on my first day I entered Colonel Beck's office and reported for duty just as people do in the movies. After I saluted, he rose and we shook hands across his desk. Then he asked me how I was and where I'd gone to medical school. When I told him the University of Tennessee, he smiled and said, 'That's where I went to school.' Colonel Beck was the most colorful and charming person at Ashford — by far the most personable officer I ever met in the Medical Department.

"Everyone on the medical staff knew everyone else, as most of our social life was with one another. I don't recall any pressure to conform to such pre-war conventions as calls on higher-ranking officers or teas at the commanding officer's home and things like that. My wife took swim lessons from the resident instructor, Charles Norelius, and we played a lot of bridge. Occasionally we drove to Lewisburg to have dinner at the General Lewis Hotel, and we went to see some of the movies shown in the hospital auditorium.

"I didn't have any direct dealings with the German POWs at Ashford, but while there I drew a related assignment: I was sent to North Africa to accompany a thousand of them to the United States. We returned to Norfolk on a Liberty ship. Such ships weren't designed to carry that many men and we were crowded beyond belief. The Army required that at least one doctor accompany every group of prisoners and treat those in need. The first day, I saw two hundred and thirty men, and worked from before daylight until ten-thirty at night.

"I also served for a short time at a small Army hospital in Elkins, West Virginia, near where Army mountain troops were trained. Some would suffer climbing accidents and they'd be brought to me to get fixed. I sent the worst cases down to Ashford by ambulance.

"For a young man starting his medical career, an assignment to Ashford was a wonderful learning opportunity. The senior staff were fine instructors and the chance to sit in a back row of the auditorium during staff meetings when treatments and case histories were discussed constituted real training. Dr. Daniel Elkin, our chief surgeon, had been at Emory; Dr. Barnes Woodhall, our top neurologist, had been at Duke; and Dr. George Prather, our chief urologist had been at Harvard. We may have had the best medical staff of any Army hospital in the United States. It was a marvelous experience, and by the time I left in April 1944, I think I'd grown a lot."

Though Dr. Corum was, as he puts it, "spared" Carlisle, and received his military indoctrination in New Orleans, many of the doctors who served at Ashford were graduates of the U.S. Army Medical Field Service School that was part of Carlisle Barracks in Carlisle, Pennsylvania. It was there that most volunteer* civilian doctors became Army doctors by virtue of completing six weeks' training in the objectives of military medicine, field sanitation, setting up evacuation hospitals, tactics, and the use of small arms. For doctors who might be assigned to forward areas, such skills were crucial.

Irving D. Harris got his M.D. degree at the University of Chicago. He enlisted in the Army in 1941, and had several assignments before being sent to White Sulphur Springs in mid-1943. After a year or so at Ashford, he was sent to the Carlisle Barracks for six weeks of training, and then served in the Philippine Islands until the war ended.

* Congress debated at length the need to draft doctors for the armed services. Those opposed to a draft argued that it would cause a severe shortage of civilian doctors. The Army alleviated its own shortage by moving its doctors away from excessive paperwork and replacing them with the non-doctors of the Medical Administrative Corps.

"At Ashford, I was a member of the Neuropsychiatric Section headed by Major E. N. Pleasants. I was a Captain then, and the other doctors in the section were John H. Iselin, Leo M. Traub, and Jerome L. Weinberger. We had eight wards on the hospital's third floor. Our patients had

The Presidential Cottage in the snow (courtesy Clinton Beuscher).

the same freedom of movement and access to the recreational facilities as any other men. We were kept quite busy, because we were getting men from every theater.

"A certain percentage of the patients were fellows who had suffered nervous breakdowns under the stress of combat. The medical staff at Ashford understood very well that such men weren't shirkers or cowards. Elsewhere, particularly among line officers, there were less sympathetic attitudes, but I never ran into any of that kind of thinking at Ashford.

"Two memories stand out for me. One of them was bumping into General Eisenhower, literally, during one of my rounds: both of us tried to squeeze through a ward door at the same time. The other was driving three golf balls in a row into Howard's Creek as other officers and VIPs watched. After that, I gave up golf for good. Altogether, though, my tour of duty at Ashford was quite pleasant."

General Eisenhower visited Ashford three times. His first visit, made somewhat reluctantly, was ordered by his boss, General George C. Marshall. On December 29, 1943, shortly before Marshall ordered Eisenhower to lead the invasion of the European continent, he sent him this brusque message:

> You will be under terrific strain from now on. I am interested that you are fully prepared to bear the strain and I am not interested in the usual responders that you can take it. It is of vast importance that you be fresh mentally and you will certainly not be if you go straight from one great problem to another. Now come home and see your wife and trust someone else for twenty minutes in England.

According to records in the Dwight D. Eisenhower Library in Abiline, Kansas, General Eisenhower arrived at Ashford with Mrs. Eisenhower on January 6, 1944. The only medical service he received was a dental exam. The general's other visits were in late 1944, and again in June 1945, when he and Mamie celebrated their 29th wedding anniversary at the hospital.

Hannah Schmutz was one of the many doctor's wives who came to Ashford with her husband. For her, born and raised only twenty-five miles away in Alderson, West Virginia, living in White Sulphur Springs was like coming home. She and her late husband, Dr. Melvin A. Schmutz, had met while she was taking nurse's training at Temple University in Philadelphia and he was in his final year of medical school there. She completed her training in 1940 and they were married. Dr. Schmutz went on active duty in March, 1944, and served in the ETO for one year before his transfer to Ashford:

"We had an enjoyable time there — it was a beautiful place, and I can easily see why writers called it a 'Shangri-La for wounded soldiers.' We lived in town with our four-year-old daughter, so our social life, in terms of attending evening affairs at the Officer's Club, was limited. We spent much of our time off, on weekends and such, in Alderson where my parents lived.

"Mel had known about the famous golf courses, and the great Sam Snead, and had asked for an assignment to White Sulphur Springs, never dreaming he'd get it. People from all over the world came to play golf at the Greenbrier. That's where he learned the game. Before his death in 1992, Mel spoke of his tour of duty at Ashford quite often."

James W. Riley was born in Eureka, Illinois, received his M.D. degree at Northwestern University in Chicago and joined the Medical Corps in mid-1943. Still single when he came to Ashford that autumn, he used his first leave to marry and move his bride to White Sulphur Springs. They lived in the Hines Apartment House, a ten-minute walk from the hospital:

"When I arrived, they were just beginning to get patients

in large numbers. I was assigned to the Orthopedics Department and reported to Major Robert P. Kelly. He's dead now, but he was a hard worker and a joy to work with. I spent long hours there, often returning after dinner at home to do some extra work around the ward. I also worked a lot of weekends. This after-hours and Saturday and Sunday work was voluntary — we didn't have to come in like that, unless we happened to draw duty as officer of the day. But with so many boys strung up in traction, I wanted to keep track of how they were doing.

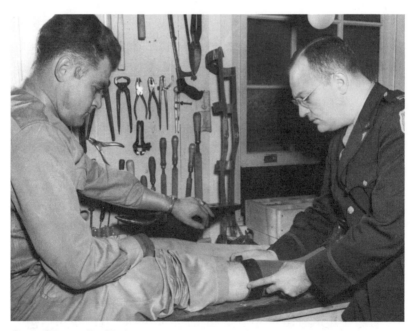

Capt. George R. Clark, a member of the Orthopedics Department, checks the leg brace of Pvt. Chester G. Badger (courtesy The Greenbrier).

"We developed a new treatment for infected arm and leg wounds that probably saved many patients months of recovery time. Since no reconstructive surgery could be performed in the presence of infection (osteomyelitis), we scraped all of the infected bone out of the cavities, then packed them with medicated gauze. A week or two later the packing was removed and a skin graft put in the clean cavity. If the graft grew, it dried up the wound and we did the reconstructive surgery. Today, skin grafts are taken for granted. Back then, they were relatively new, made possible only by the sulpha drugs and penicillin.

"I also helped care for some of the German prisoners of war who had their own sick bay at the hospital. Many were really handsome fellows, tanned and rugged — *Afrika Korps* soldiers who'd been captured in Tunisia. One came in with gonorrhea. When I inquired how he got it, he said he'd seduced a hotel employee in an elevator. Those Germans had it made there: they ate well and got plenty of outdoor work. No way did any of them want to escape!

"My wife and I were pretty young when we were at Ashford — I was only twenty-eight — and just starting out in life. We didn't have a car. And we weren't exactly part of the social whirl. That was pretty much an Emory University crowd, and pretty cliquish too. You didn't break into that too easily, especially the young doctors and wives. If you didn't agree that the Emory people were the greatest doctors in the world and knew their whiskey, you didn't last long.

"Colonel Beck was a fine entertainer, a handsome man, and a good administrator. I call him an 'entertainer' only in the sense that he was able to put on a good show for those high-ranking visitors coming to see the Army's showcase hospital.I really don't know how good a doctor he was. Many old-line Medical Corps officers had held administrative positions so long they weren't aware of recent medical breakthroughs.

"The Surgeon General, Major General Norman T. Kirk, once came for a visit. Most of the younger doctors wrote papers to present at a seminar. I gave something on the treatment of fractures of the upper arm and received many compliments on it, including one from Kirk. I think the paper was published in *The Annals of Surgery* and *The Army Medical Journal*.

"Everybody was scared to death of General Kirk. He was an ornery so-and-so but quite competent. If you crossed him, or did something to a patient that wasn't standard, you stood a good chance of being reassigned to the 'boondocks.'

"We got to know a few townspeople. One of them was Captain R.H. Patterson, who had been the Greenbrier's head engineer. He'd been given the commission in order to retain him in that position. We also met the Gillespies, who lived across from us, above their flower shop.

"One of the Gillespie girls had a very painful hip. Since none of the local doctors seemed able to diagnose what was wrong with her, I was asked to try. I brought her into the hospital one night, and arranged to have her X-rayed. She had what we call 'Legg-Perthes' disease and needed to have an immediate operation. I sent her to a surgeon in Roanoke, and after she had fully recovered, I believe she eventually walked normally.

"Some of my patients were real hillbillies. When I picked up my morning paper at the basement news stand, there always seemed to be tons of comic books, and these fellows from the hills would grab them in preference to everything else. Some of those boys — and they surely weren't all West Virginians — would go to sleep with plugs of chewing tobacco jammed in their cheeks. It's a wonder they didn't strangle.

"I used the swimming pool a lot, but not voluntarily. They said we had to learn to swim, and I was required to attend classes three times a week. I drank half the water in that pool and almost drowned, but never learned to swim. Still can't. I met both the fabulous Esther Williams and Walter Pidgeon, a grand fellow. He had the worst complexion I've ever seen on a man — terrible acne scars. I can't imagine how makeup ever covered them. But he was a heck of an actor and one of the most popular stars to visit Ashford.

Ashford's Orthopedics staff: front l. to r., Lt. Robert Murray, Maj. Robert P. Kelly, Capt. James W. Riley; rear, l. to r., Capt. Rossati, Capt. Paul L. Reith, Capt. Ernie Burgess (courtesy Dr. James Riley).

"I also met General Eisenhower when he came in for a visit, and Mamie, too. I think 'Ike' spent more time fishing than he did golfing, but they say he didn't do so well. It seems all the big trout had been spoiled by GIs throwing popcorn to them, and they weren't hungry enough to rise to hand-tied flies anymore.

"I wasn't a bad golfer and played once or twice a week whenever I had time. My wife and I often dined and went to dances at the Officer's Club. The bartender's name was

'Boz,' and he was a big, genial fellow who taught me to make eggnog richer by putting in about a quart of ice cream. We had some nice steak dinners (probably 'black market') at a place called the Eagle's Nest, a mountainside tavern some miles east of White Sulphur Springs.

"We've been back to the Greenbrier several times, It's still the greatest place but just a little expensive unless you go representing somebody who will pay the tab. The town hasn't changed much, and I doubt that it ever will. Our experiences there are unforgettable."

On visits to Ashford, General and Mrs. Eisenhower usually stayed at "Top Notch," a large free-standing cottage built in 1912 on a high point just above the hospital's main buildings. It was there, on the front porch, that "Ike" sat for a bust by the popular sculptor Archimedes Giacomantonio. The original is now displayed in the United States Military Academy Museum at West Point, and a bronze copy can be seen in The Greenbrier's North Parlor.

Corporal Giacomantonio, called "Jocko" by his friends in the Special Service unit, was assigned to Ashford to help plastic surgeons in reconstructive surgery. In 1975, he wrote to The Greenbrier's Historian, Dr. Robert Conte, about working with General Eisenhower:

> This was the first sculpture he had ever posed for. We spent seven days working on the clay model. We chatted about many subjects. His wife Mamie and son John would join in the conversations. . . .

> The general was aware of his wide "peripheral view," better known as exotropia. This means his eyes pointed a little to the left and right instead of straight ahead. He had a habit of speaking out of the side of his mouth. He tried to correct this. The right side of his head was more devel-

oped than the left side, evidenced by two small lines over his right eyebrow. I noticed the lack of sideburns in front of his ears. He said, "They just never grew." His skull was massive and he wore an oversized hat.

[The] three sittings that I originally requested turned out to be seven because he wanted to see this project completed in his presence. He gave me the extra sittings and cooperated to the fullest extent.

Archimedes Giacomantonio and General Eisenhower with the clay model fashioned during Ike's stay at Top Notch Cottage (courtesy The Greenbrier).

After becoming a civilian again, Giacomantonio went on to win considerable acclaim for his artistry. In response to an unexpected gift he'd sent to the Eisenhowers just before the presidential election of 1952, Mrs. Eisenhower thanked him and expressed her great satisfaction with his work:

The General and I were just delighted to receive the record you sent us of the song you composed about him. We look forward to playing it soon, for we think the lyrics are excellent indeed! We have often spoken about those pleasant days you spent in our home in White Sulphur Springs when you were carving a bust of the General. That likeness was one of the finest I have ever seen!

Bronislava Z. Reznick, a native of Russia, earned her M.D. degree at St. Vladimir University in Kiev. She came to the U.S. in 1923, and completed her residency at North Chicago Hospital. Dr. Reznick became an American citizen and began her own practice in 1929. In mid-1943, she joined the Army Medical Corps with the rank of captain and was assigned to Camp Crowder, Missouri. Female Army doctors were a rarity, and some amusing things happened because she persisted in using her initials rather than her first name. After her assignment at Lawson General Hospital in Atlanta, she was sent to Ashford on May 5, 1944:

"I was assigned there when they needed an eye, ear, nose and throat specialist. We had an examination clinic, as well as a tiny operating room on the fifth floor for tonsilectomies, bronchoscopies, and minor eye surgeries. We used the regular operating rooms for more complicated surgery. Ophthalmology was my field. Though my memory is presently not so good, it seems to me that we were kept pretty busy.

"However, I did have time for golfing, which I enjoyed very much. Sometimes I would play a round all by myself, taking my time to look at the beautiful green hills that surrounded White Sulphur Springs. The German prisoners — the Nazis — who took care of the greens and fairways seemed to be having a very nice time, indeed. Being Russian-born, I was not too fond of them."

The Eye, Ears, Nose, and Throat (EENT) Clinic mainly treated patients whose eyes and ears had been damaged by shrapnel or exploding bombs and shells. Major Cecil B. Hert was the chief of otolaryngology. Major John M. Masters, was the chief of ophthalmology. Captain Leo J. Croll was EENT ward officer. Two nurses and a number of enlisted men completed the staff.

Frederick M. Stark, M.D., calls himself a late "conscript" to the U.S. Army. Following his Carlisle "graduation" on November 17, 1944, and short assignments to Mason General Hospital (Brentwood, Long Island) and Northington General Hospital (Tuscaloosa, Alabama), he was ordered to White Sulphur Springs in January 1945:

"At Ashford, I was in the neurologic service working under Major Ralph W. Barris, M.D., who had come from the Scripps Metabolic Clinic in California. Captain William Engstrom was also in the neurologic service. My best friend at the hospital was Captain Kaden Tierney, also a doctor. Colonel Clare T. Budge, the head of the dental clinic, was another splendid chap and, like me, a real golf nut.

' "In April 1945, I took a short leave to be married to Alice Palmer of Hamilton, Ontario. We both found Ashford totally beautiful. What a great place for a honeymoon!

"Occasionally I played golf with a Corporal Petroske, who'd been a golf pro in Connecticut. I felt that we were pretty evenly matched, so we played for money. He usually nosed me out, particularly if I suggested going for double or nothing on the last hole. Finally, I owed him one hundred and eighty dollars and was fortunate that he settled for fifty cents on the dollar, or ninety dollars. Since then I've never played for more than nickels and dimes.

"There was a nearby camp for German prisoners, and some of them worked on the golf courses. If they found lost balls they sold them to Army personnel, who paid up in cash even though the POWs were never supposed to have U.S. currency. One evening we saw a German waiting on the golf course for the truck back to his camp. He was practicing chip shots with a nine-iron."

Winners of Fifth Service Command golf tourney receive trophy. From left: Col. Clyde Beck, Pfc. Quintin Stewart, Cpl. Pete Petroske, Lt. Frederick Stark, and Major Gen. James Collins, who made the presentation (courtesy Dr. Frederick Stark).

Everyone remembers the German prisoners, but the Italians who preceded them made little impression. They stayed for a shorter time, and had fewer opportunities for direct contact with anyone other than their guards. The Italians arrived at Camp Ashford in time to be employed by local farmers to help with the 1943 harvest, but none seemed to have worked at the hospital.

Joseph C. Justo, born in Birmingham, Alabama, was one of the hospital's several post veterinarians. He joined the

Medical Administrative Corps straight from the veterinary college at Auburn University. After a transfer to the Veterinary Corps, First Lt. Justo held assignments in Kansas City, Indianapolis, and Greensboro, North Carolina, before being sent to Ashford in the autumn of 1945:

"The veterinarian's principal job throughout the Army was to assure the good quality of the meat and dairy products that the Army purchased for its officers and men. In World War I, as in most wars, unscrupulous suppliers were notorious for tricking the Army into buying bad meat or even switching bad for good after the sale was made. Some packers were known to inject chickens with cheap mineral oil so they weighed more, or to substitute tough old roosters for tender hens. At Ashford, we had none of that because

First Lieutenant Joseph C. Justo, Ashford Hospital veterinarian, and friend.

every shipment was checked before and after it was delivered. Most of our dairy products were bought from local dairymen, who gave us nothing but completely wholesome foodstuffs.

"I was single at that time, so they housed me in one of the cottages, where I had quarters to myself. Just before the hospital closed, I was moved into one of the barracks that the WACs had moved out of. I don't recall going down

The prisoner of war who helped Dr. Justo in his work with animals in the stables area.

to the stable area much, but I know that two mules and a few sheep were kept there. I think they were 'blooded' and the blood used to make certain serums. I didn't have any help at the end, just one 'German' prisoner of war — who was really an Austrian captured by the Germans and made to fight for them. We got along just fine.

"We once had a big food poisoning scare. The first to get sick were some of the morning shift cooks who probably ate some leftovers. Then some nurses coming on to day duty got sick. Food poisoning was a huge threat because of all the men in weakened condition who would have small resistance to its effects. I discovered the source of the problem at once: some cooked hams had been left out all night without refrigeration. General Beck commended me for nipping the situation in the bud."

Post veterinarians sometimes also examined and provided care for the dogs owned by Ashford personnel. Some of the dogs, like the commandant's Doberman pinscher, "Red," had belonged to enemy diplomats, who had not been allowed to take animals home with them when they were repatriated. Other dogs were strays like "Bootsie," the little white-haired dog the Cadet Nurses adopted as their mascot. When he wandered off, his place was taken by "Murphy," another stray.

Arthur N. Kracht graduated from the Northwestern University Dental College in 1933, and entered active duty in the Army the following year. By the time he was assigned to Ashford in November 1942, he was a veteran Army dental officer. At Ashford, he planned and guided the construction of its well-equipped dental clinic, and was Chief of the Dental Service until early 1944:

"I got to White Sulphur Springs shortly after the hospital opened. Three big-time architectural firms got most of the work of converting the hotel to a hospital. I remember how the medical doctors jockeyed for the best space. They had the priority, and so our nine-chair Dental Clinic wound up on the lower level in what had been the hotel's paint shop.

"By late 1943, we had twelve chairs, an ample waiting room, and we could do everything from preparing dentures, bridges and splints to treating fractures, cysts, abscesses, tumors and other diseases of the mouth. I had two captains, John P. Rohrbaugh and Leo J. Chamness, as my chief assistants. Miss Jean Pauls — a terrific gal — was our civilian hygienist. Two other dentists, First Lieutenants Robert Reed and Bernard Schneider, and nine dental technicians completed the staff.

"After Ashford, I served in the 140th Evacuation Hospital and then the 8th (later redesignated the 108th) Evacuation Hospital. I served as plans and training officer for both hospitals. This was unpleasant duty, but it helped prepare me for the teaching I'd do after the war. Eventually I was assigned to the 16th Armored Division and remained with it through V-E Day. Looking back, I think of my Ashford days as having been interesting — perhaps the best of my whole Army career."

Overseas duty in combat zones was hard on a GI's dental health. There was ample reason: fewer chances for brushing, brushes lost and never replaced, infections left untreated, and diseases spread via shared eating and drinking utensils. Many of the patients who came to Ashford for quite different types of treatments also turned up in the Dental Clinic for professional cleaning and various dental repairs. Some men probably had never been in a dentist's chair before.

Joseph J. Bruno, a 1931 Yale graduate, got his M.D. degree at Hahnemann University Medical School in Philadelphia. He joined the Medical Corps in May 1941, and served in various field hospitals in the Pacific theater between January 1942 and May 1943. After returning to the States, Capt. Bruno served at Ashford from August 1943 until October 1944:

"There I was assigned as the medical officer at the prisoner of war camp. I headed a small group of enlisted men from the medical detachment and we ran the camp dispensary. We took care of any illness that didn't require hospitalization and the more serious cases were taken to Ashford. First there were Italian POWs, then German.

Capt. Joseph J. Bruno, M.D., with German POWs outside the camp clinic, February 1944.

"I understood both Italian and German, and I managed quite well, although I did need an interpreter occasionally, and had help from a German prisoner who was a doctor. The German POWs worked every day in and around the hospital. I found them to be clean, and quite clever in how they adapted to their surroundings. Most were well-behaved, and troublemakers were transferred to another camp.

"One event that I recall rather vividly was when an MP shot one of the prisoners just as he was leaving the compound on a work detail. This particular guard was a combat veteran who had replaced one of the MPs we'd had from the beginning. Apparently he was 'edgy' about the Germans but exactly what happened I don't know. We rushed the wounded man to Ashford where he made a full recovery. Generally speaking, our MPs handled everything extremely well, and there were never any real problems.

"After my previous field assignments (including service on Guadalcanal), Ashford was very pleasant. I saw some movies, swam in the indoor pool, attended Officer's Club dances, and sometimes took part in the prison camp staff parties held in White Sulphur Springs. My wife and my two little girls came down once, and we rented a cabin in the woods for two weeks. After being in the Pacific so long, it was wonderful to have my family around me again.

"I greatly enjoyed my duties at Ashford, and my association with doctors from other parts of the country. Though I've always wanted to go back to see what the hotel looks like now, I never have. After nearly half a century I still have many pleasant memories of Ashford."

Charles E. Magner grew up in Montana, won the state amateur golf championship when he was nineteen, earned an M.D. from the University of Chicago, and in May 1942 entered the Army Medical Corps. After two years as a battalion surgeon with the Alaska Scouts in the Aleutian Campaign, he transferred to the paratroops. On his eleventh training jump, he injured his left knee and was hospitalized for three months. Placed on permanent limited duty, Dr. Magner was ordered to Ashford General Hospital in March 1945:

"I was assigned to the 'officer's wing' as an assistant to Dr. Daniel C. Elkin. Part of that job entailed maintaining a dozen beds for visiting VIPs. In that way, I met Generals Eisenhower, Wainwright, McAuliffe, and many others. I spent much of my time with the Officer's Retirement Board getting officers out of service, a task that speeded up markedly as the war wound down and then ended.

First Lt. Charles Magner, M.D., in the Aleutians with his pet eagle and a skull found deep in the frozen tundra.

"But I also performed surgery and one of my first cases was a real surprise. A group of ten or twelve new patients had been checked in and I was reviewing their EMTs — emergency medical treatment tags — when I was stopped in my tracks by some very familiar handwriting. It was my own. I had treated the boy long before in the Aleutians. He'd had a severe head wound and I'd removed a lot of his damaged brain tissue with a sterilized bent spoon. I didn't think he could live. But he'd been shipped back to a hospital in Pennsylvania and pulled through.

"He survived, I believe, because the wound was so large that no pressure ever built up, and none of the rest of the brain was destroyed. He still needed restorative surgery to fit a protective plate over a large depression in his skull, and I put in a tantalum plate. Such an operation requires taking a wax impression of the region to be covered and then having a mold made from it. The malleable tantalum metal is shaped to make an exact fit, then attached to the cranium and covered with skin. I can't attest to the boy's intelligence before he was wounded, but he apparently did well in his recovery.

"At Ashford, we had time to play golf with visiting VIPs and that was quite pleasant. I played with 'Ike' and with Tony McAuliffe, the famous Battle of the Bulge general who's said to have replied 'Nuts!' to the German commander who demanded his surrender. Only McAuliffe told me that he hadn't really said that. He'd said something that his translator had such difficulty putting into German that, angered by his lack of skill, the man just blurted out, 'Ah nuts!'

"I also played golf with Ernest DeBakey, one of our general and thoracic surgeons and brother of the famous Dr. Michael DeBakey. Ernest was an excellent golfer, but had a terrible temper. Out practicing his drives one day, he hit an awful slice, then a topper, than another slice. After each shot he turned and smiled. We couldn't believe his calm. He was getting ready to drive again when it exploded. He threw the club, the ball, the tee, and his golf bag right in Howard's Creek, and stomped angrily back to the clubhouse. The next day he hired a caddy to retrieve his clubs and bag.

"Some congressman once came to the hospital demanding a bed in the officer's wing and suggesting that I move out a dying lieutenant to make room. He also wanted some of the original mineral water for which the Greenbrier was famous. Well, the original spring is situated in a neglected wooded area above the hotel, not down at the Springhouse.

Capt. Charles Magner, M.D.

"I knew how to find it from a map I'd seen in the hotel museum. Removing some twigs and leaves and dead frogs, I filled a gallon bottle with the smelly water and placed it in the ice box as the congressman had asked. I don't know how much he drank but for three days he had God-awful diarrhea.

"I never took leave during my year and a half at Ashford. I didn't need one — just being there was a vacation. I loved to fish, and Howard's Creek was stocked with trout from the fish hatchery in White Sulphur Springs. Gear was provided by the hospital. I'd noticed that the trout had learned to eat popcorn thrown to them by strollers, so I arranged this fishing contest with some of my friends, each of us putting some cash into a pool for the winners. Well, I caught more trout in fifteen minutes than the rest did in the half-hour limit. When they protested against my using popcorn in lieu of proper flies, I stood everyone a drink and refunded half their entry fee.

"I met Mamie Eisenhower and worked with her on plans for the general's grand return from Europe after V-E Day. She was a great lady. Colonels Beck and Elkin also were tops. I didn't socialize much, other than at the Officer's Club, and on the golf courses. My sergeant drove me out in the hills once to visit a moonshiner. I brought back a quart to the Officer's Club, and treated some friends to a round. I poured each of them about three fingers, and the faces they made after they swallowed it were something to see. That's why it's called 'white lightning,' I guess.

"I was separated from the service at Ashford on August 4, 1946. I'd had enough of Army life by then. I can't play golf anymore because of my arthritis, and I've never been back to the Greenbrier, but I have a lot of happy memories of it."

The Greenbrier's first eighteen-hole golf course, known for years simply as the Number One Course, and later as the Old White Course, was opened in 1913. Designed by Charles Blair McDonald, who was considered the greatest authority on golf architecture in America, the 6,250-yard course was named by *Town and Country* magazine as being among the country's best. A second eighteen-hole course, named The Greenbrier, opened in 1924. The nine-hole Number Two Course was built between the two longer courses and, during the Ashford Hospital years it was reserved for beginners.

Golf and The Greenbrier have always been synonomous. From the 1920s up through the 1950s, almost all of America's most famous professional golfers played there — among them Bobby Jones, Walter Hagen, Ben Hogan, Gene Sarazen, and Sam Snead. Before golf came to The Greenbrier itself, "Oakhurst," which many accept as the first golf club in the United States, was established in 1884 on an estate only a few miles from the Greenbrier. Though disbanded after a decade, "Oakhurst" was the site of annual meets, and the club awarded a "Challenge Medal" to the winners.

Ernest G. DeBakey joined the Army Air Corps Reserve in his senior year of medical school. Following graduation, he was called to active duty and sent to flight surgeon's school at Randolph Field, Texas. Eventually, he joined a squadron in the China-Burma-India theater that was flying supplies from India to China over the Himalayas ("the hump") in C-46s and C-54s. His tour completed, he was rotated back to Florida, where he began to seek duty that would make more use of his surgical skills:

"I wanted to get out of the Air Force and into the Army. My brother Michael was then in the Surgeon General's Office in Washington, DC, working under Brigadier General Fred Rankin. I told my brother I wanted to come and talk with him about a transfer. Michael was just leaving for France, but arranged an interview with General Rankin.

"When I got there, the general was sitting at his desk, and, as a mere major, I was scared to death. Hearing me out, he asked 'Where'd you like to go?' I said 'I don't know, sir, wherever you want to send me.' He had a big wall map at his back, and he told me to consider all the hospitals on it and pick my spot. I saw this dot at White Sulphur Springs and I said 'Sir, it would be mighty nice if I could go there.' I'd never seen it, but I knew of the Greenbrier. I was delighted when the general had my transfer orders cut immediately.

"As it happened, I didn't get much of the kind of surgery I wanted to do. Mostly I removed the tantalum plates placed over damaged nerves by the surgeons who'd first made

Ernest G. DeBakey, M.D., served in the China-Burma-India theater for over a year before coming to Ashford.

the repairs. I wasn't very busy, but that was all right. It gave me time to play a lot of golf. Though I wasn't an expert, no matter what anyone may say, I had an eight or a nine handicap, and that's pretty good.

"We did have some experts. My colleague, Dr. Charles Magner, was certainly one of them. He and a couple of other amateurs there used to play two former professionals. It was usually touch and go. The amateurs would win one match, the pros the next. As little by little, the pros proved to be the better players, I quit betting on the matches.

"Our commanding officer, Colonel Beck, was an avid golfer. We'd take note of when he left his office every afternoon to head for the clubhouse. Thirty minutes later, we'd follow in his footsteps. A frequent civilian guest was Dr. Gory Hogg, who'd been a golf club member from before the war, and whom Colonel Beck graciously allowed to continue his daily round. Nearly eighty years old, Dr. Hogg was a remarkable man, and had been golfing at the Greenbrier for most of forty years. He was still making some fine shots when I played with him.

"I did have a temper in those days, just as Dr. Magner says. One of my two-irons probably is still hanging in one of the trees down there! I didn't play tennis or use the swimming pool, but I well remember the Officer's Club where we played poker and the slot machines, and were served by German POWs. I've never been back to the Greenbrier, but I have many fine memories of the men and women who served at Ashford General Hospital."

The tantalum mentioned by Dr. DeBakey was as much a "miracle metal" as penicillin was a "miracle drug." Surgeons used it extensively in the repair of patients who had suffered nerve and cranial injuries. Resistant to chemical attack, tantalum was used in the form of wire, foil, and plates that could be left inside the body without fear of corrosion. Though hard and heavy, the metal could be drawn into suture wire as fine as three-thousandths of an inch.

Harry B. Durham grew up in Casper, Wyoming, and earned his M.D. degree at Northwestern University. In June 1945, after finishing his internship, he enlisted in the Medical Corps. He was indoctrinated at Carlisle Barracks, and trained for an additional six weeks at the Army's School for Personnel Services before his assignment to Ashford:

"A number of us at Carlisle were chosen to go to Lexington, Virginia to learn about reconditioning programs. These went beyond physical rehabilitation by introducing an educational component. At Ashford, we called that 'exercising the brain cells.' We felt it was extremely important to keep men up to date on world news and to help them improve their educations through Armed Forces Institute courses and classes conducted right at the hospital. I was the only medical officer in the program and trained the technicians who did the actual work.

"All of the various sports activities were included under reconditioning: golf, basketball, volleyball, softball, the whole works. Of course, this was after the war, and things were winding down, so I had lots of free time myself. Since golf was one of the reconditioning activities and I'd never played, I got into it a little. We used to kid that we had to play every day to check that the flags were in place.

"My wife and I rented an apartment in town. Housing was so scarce that many townspeople converted some of the rooms in their single-family homes into small flats. Mrs. Beck and other ladies welcomed my wife as a new lady on the post but we weren't too involved socially because we were only there for six months or so. We had a car and sometimes drove over to Roanoke for dinner. My wife's uncle lived in Charleston so we drove there for a visit and enjoyed beautiful scenery along the way.

"The White Sulphur Springs townspeople were at times

a bit stand-offish. This may have been a carryover from years of being somewhat ignored: certainly the townspeople and the Greenbrier's wealthy guests had seldom mixed. Folks weren't unfriendly, just a little aloof. Some xenophobia also may have been involved. My wife and I haven't been back, but we'd really like to go and see how everything looks today."

The Armed Forces Institute (AFI) referred to by Dr. Durham gave servicemen and women an opportunity to sign up for any one of sixty-four courses of study for only $2 each. Those who took courses for college credit from a participating college would pay half the cost and the Army the other half. Enrollees worked at their own pace. In three years, nearly three thousand Ashford patients and staff took AFI courses.

Gustavus A. Peters, from the Indianapolis, Indiana area, earned his M.D. degree at the University of Indiana, then took additional training in physical medicine at the Mayo Clinic. After joining the Medical Corps in late 1944, he trained at Carlisle Barracks and Fort McClellan, Alabama, and after some temporary assignments, reported to Ashford General Hospital in November 1945:

"The Army said I could practice either internal medicine or physical medicine, since I'd specialized in both. I felt my better contribution would result from staying with physical medicine, which dealt with physical and occupational therapy and rehabilitation. So at Ashford, I headed the section that did those things. I avoided hands-on work, largely because members of my staff were better trained for that than I was. By virtue of daily experience, they gradually honed their skills, something I wouldn't have had time for.

"My wife and I leased an apartment in White Sulphur Springs, along Howard's Creek, and our first child was born while we lived there. It was too far to walk, so I drove in to the hospital each day. We took some weekend jaunts to Virginia and I'm sure we drove to Roanoke for dinner, saw the famous Natural Bridge, and that sort of thing. Serving as a doctor at Ashford was almost the same as remaining a civilian."

Dr. Gustavus A. Peters was among the hundreds who watched golfers Byron Nelson and Sam Snead pair off to play against Skii Riegel and Jimmy Demaret on April 10, 1946.

The goal of physical therapy was to prepare men either to return to active duty or to go home. The hospital's Physical Therapy Section used every tool at its disposal. In addition to the swimming pool and special baths, there were heat lamps and cabinets, massage tables, short wave diathermy machines, ultraviolet lamps, special electrical machines for studying and treating paralyzed nerves, and two fever cabinets. Many mechanical devices were used to stretch and exercise muscles and joints. Significant advances were made in all aspects of physical therapy throughout the war.

An integral part of the reconditioning program, described in a hospital-produced brochure, "The Royal Road to Recovery," was calisthentics. On sunny days, groups of up to 150 men could be seen exercising in cadence on the lawn

Cover of a Special Services brochure describing the purposes and opportunities for physical rehabilitation at Ashford. The men are doing the Army's "side straddle hop" on the North lawn (courtesy Maxine Justice).

in front of the hospital's north entrance. On rainy days, the patients did their bending and stretching in the gym.

The difficulty of the exercises assigned depended on the men's abilities. Class IV (bed patients) did exercises in bed and used only the lightweight equipment brought to them on a mobile "Muscle Cart." Class III (ambulatory patients) were subdivided into four groups: Class III BE men received physical reconditioning in the wards, even though they were ambulatory; Class III BR men took remedial exercises in the "remedial gym" near the swimming pool; Class III B patients were allowed all physical activities except swimming; Class III A patients could participate in any physical activity.

Erich Steiner was working toward his Ph.D. in biology at the University of Virginia when he was called to active service. Steiner completed the Medical Administrative Corps OCS, and was commissioned in May 1945. Following weeks of temporary duty at hospitals in Memphis and Atlanta, he was ordered to the Army School for Personnel Services at Washington and Lee University in Lexington, Virginia. After finishing the six-week course, 1st Lt. Steiner was sent to Ashford. He and his wife Dotty were pleased to be going to White Sulphur Springs because it was near her family's home in Roanoke.

"Finding housing at a new post was always a problem. Dotty was given an address by folks at the hospital, and rented a room in what once must have been a grand home. Though the room was large and it had a nice bay window, its furnishings were sparce: an old brass bed, some straight-backed chairs, and a well-worn linoleum floor. The fireplace was sealed off, and a bare light bulb dangled from the ceiling. The bathroom tub was unique. Even a six-footer could stretch out full length in it. I've never seen one like it since.

"Those accommodations might have proved tolerable had it not been for the bats that also lived there. They were the last straw. 'Making do' was one thing. Trying to sleep with bats flitting about the room was quite another, and so Dotty went door to door in search of another place to live. That's how we came to the Gillespies.

First Lt. Erich Steiner and his wife, Dotty, out for a stroll along Howard's Creek.

"Ken Gillespie was the Mayor of White Sulphur Springs, and before the war he'd operated the Greenbrier's flower shop. In our time, his flower shop was in the town. I believe that their son was away then, and they rented us his room; it was comfortable and cozy, and we felt completely at home. We all became friends and when, in a few weeks, they told us of a vacancy in their apartment house, we grabbed it.

"My assignment at Ashford General was in the educational reconditioning program. When I arrived, my duties were ill-defined. I spent time a lot of time with patients, learning their backgrounds, and their plans for returning to civilian life. It was obvious that few would return to duty, and that many would be sent home with disabilities. I began to feel that I could do something useful by developing a vocational counseling service for men soon to be discharged.

"We assembled various Armed Forces Institute materials and formed a small library of vocational information. We also administered tests designed to determine levels of ability for higher education and training, and special aptitudes or interests that could be related to particular vocations. I was much interested in these activities and grateful that I was able to do something valuable for soon-to-be veterans.

"Since the war was over, the work pace was relaxed. I would often go to lunch early with a fellow officer and then play nine holes of golf. Back in my office by mid-afternoon, I'd still have time to finish my work before the end of the day. Although Dotty had her college degree in home economics, she took a job teaching eighth grade math and science at a local school.

"So, by the end of the year we were both happily employed, had a comfortable apartment, and were enjoying good friends. We had every reason to think we'd be at Ashford a long time. We were stunned when I was ordered to Newport News to serve aboard the *Rensselaer Victory*, a troopship bringing our men home from Europe.

"Fortunately, between sailings I was able to arrange for a position with the Veterans Administration in Roanoke, and was officially separated from the Army in May, 1946. Though Dotty and I only lived there for a short time, we have many fond memories of our days in White Sulphur Springs."

Brig. Gen. Beck introducing members of his staff to General Jonathan Wainwright (at far left) (courtesy The Greenbrier).

The School for Personnel Services (originally called the Special Service School) was established to teach officers and enlisted men how to maintain troop morale. Toward the end of the war, it offered programs directed toward helping millions of returning veterans fit into civilian life again. In the four years of its existence, the school at Lexington graduated more than 18,000 officers and men, about 2,200 of them specializing in education and vocational counseling.

Many soldiers had entered service with limited educational and employment experience. For them, learning skills that would be useful in civilian life was important. A classic example was Pvt. Russell P. Dalton who had been wounded in his left wrist and shoulder and slightly less seriously in his right hand. After four months at Ashford, Pvt. Dalton signed up for typing lessons. Using only his right hand, he was soon writing letters and thinking about a career in business. Other patients studied everything from drafting to motor mechanics.

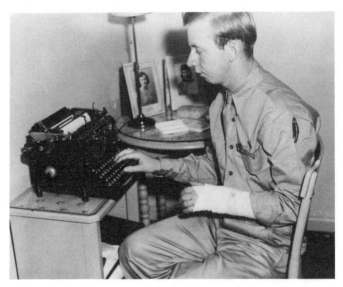

Pvt. Russel P. Dalton of Big Island, Virginia, learning the hunt and peck system of typing, using only his right hand (courtesy J.W. Benjamin, Jr.).

Jesse E. Thompson was born and raised in Texas, but earned his M.D. degree at Harvard University. After completing his residency at Massachusetts General Hospital he practiced four years of what he calls "academic surgery" in Boston. At Massachusetts General, he took training in neurosurgery, and became greatly interested in vascular surgery as well. When he entered the Army in 1945 his assigned military occupation speciality was in neurosurgery. After training at Carlisle, 1st Lt. Thompson seemed destined to head to the Pacific, but then the first atomic bomb was dropped:

"At which point, all orders changed, and everybody went to unexpected places. I was sent to White Sulphur Springs and Ashford General Hospital. Since the war was over, the Army was discharging many of its veteran doctors and looking for replacements. My neurosurgery speciality undoubtedly got me to Ashford.

"We were very busy, because we still were getting patients from Europe, and many transferees from other hospitals all over the United States. I performed both neurosurgery and vascular surgery. I was there from the autumn of 1945 until the hospital was closed in June 1946. Most of the remaining patients, along with myself and many other doctors, went to Walter Reed Army Hospital. I was discharged there in 1947.

"The surgical staff at Ashford was outstanding. Many had held teaching positions at Emory University in Atlanta. In fact, there were so many ex-Emory men at Ashford we called them the 'EPA,' or Emory Protection Association. We joked about it because, while so many doctors passed through the hospital on their way overseas, the Emory men always seemed to stay put in beautiful White Sulphur Springs.

"There weren't any classroom sessions for the doctors at Ashford but it was still very much a learning situation. I was a young surgeon then, and glad to have such experienced doctors to follow about on rounds. I learned a lot just in hearing cases discussed. There was always a diversity that we would never see in our private practices.

"I was married when I was assigned to West Virginia, and my wife and I had a little girl. We lived in the village just a short walk from the hospital. There wasn't much going on in town, and I didn't learn much about it. We shopped at a local market for some groceries, but we bought most things in the hospital PX. There was a state-run liquor store in town, and a movie house, but we had plenty of activities on the hospital campus — golfing, swimming, and such.

"When I went into the Greenbrier itself, I was flabber-gasted by the beauty of the place. I was really never so surprised in my life, and my wife had the same reaction. At the train station, I'd asked someone where Ashford was and they'd said 'Right over there under the trees, just walk right in!' The place didn't look like any hospital I'd ever seen. My wife and I have returned many times and the buildings and grounds are more lovely than ever."

Brig. Gen. Clyde Beck offering fried chicken "seconds" to guests at an Officer's Club dinner dance (courtesy Erich Steiner).

William C. Fitzpatrick went to the Indiana University School of Dentistry and upon graduation in 1943 was com-missioned in the Dental Corps. He spent eighteen months "on the amalgam line" at Camp Breckenridge, Kentucky, helping to prepare the 82nd Airborne Division for overseas duty. From there he went to Fletcher General Hospital in Cambridge, Ohio, where most of his patients were soldiers just back from overseas:

"I was promoted to captain at Fletcher General, and a year later was transferred to Ashford General, getting there in early 1946. Again I only did fillings while older and more experienced dentists did the extractions and reconstructive surgery. We all used novacaine as our injection anesthetic and didn't use any general anesthesia such as laughing gas. We also had a prosthetics section where patients who lacked their teeth were fitted with full dentures. Few 'partials' or bridges were made.

"My wife and two young children joined me in White Sulphur Springs, and we rented an apartment in town, coincidentally right over a dentist's office. The apartment had no carpets and our second child, who was a mere toddler, had a wooden-wheeled walker that he trundled back and forth over squeaky hardwood floors. I don't know how Dr. Krickenberger stood it, but he never complained.

"My wife and I became interested in the many springs in that part of Virginia and West Virginia and tried to find as many as possible. Some of the older springs were overgrown and in ruins, but many were still going strong. It was also fun to learn about the Greenbrier itself.

"We had patients to treat until mid-summer. Then the Dental Clinic just closed up shop. All the dental officers left and I was still hanging around with nothing to do. Finally, and rather sheepishly, the Army admitted it had misplaced orders for me to proceed to Fort Benjamin Harrison, Indiana, for my discharge. I'm sorry I had so little time at Ashford."

Once hostilities ceased, the beautiful hospital in peaceful little White Sulphur Springs became a mecca for all sorts of visiting "brass." From June 1945 through June 1946, sixty-four generals, often accompanied by their wives, visited the hospital for medical check-ups. Among them were Eisenhower, Bradley, McAuliffe, Wainwright, Clark, Ridgway, and Louis B. Hershey, wartime director of the Selective Service System.

On September 19, 1945, Gen. Jonathan Wainwright, "The Hero of Bataan," who was a Japanese captive for over three years, became a patient at Ashford. One week earlier, four million people had cheered his "welcome home" parade down New York's Fifth Avenue. On his first evening at Ashford, the general spoke on NBC radio about his years as a prisoner, and about receiving the Medal of Honor.

General Jonathan Wainwright broadcasts to the nation from "secret location" at Ashford (courtesy J.W. Benjamin, Jr.).

Wainwright and his wife were guests at the hospital for six weeks, staying in Top Notch Cottage and frequently dining with Gen. and Mrs. Beck. On one occasion, Gen. Wainwright visited the White Sulphur Springs High School to speak at a student assembly, where he was given a real hero's welcome,

Morton Galdston grew up in the Bronx, New York, and earned his M.D. degree at New York University Medical Center. He joined the Medical Corps in April 1943, and after training at Carlisle Barracks went to Lovell General Hospital, Fort Devens, Massachusetts. Just as he was about to be named chief of medicine, he was sent to the Chemical Warfare Research Center at Edgewood Arsenal, Maryland. In February 1946, Dr. Galdston was ordered to Ashford, and became Chief of the General Medicine Section and consultant to the other medical services:

"Going to Ashford was a wonderful change for me. We were then mainly receiving men with service-related and chronic illnesses, and acting as a clearing house, discharging them to the Veterans Hospitals nearest their homes. The hospital was not terribly busy, but clearly winding down and soon to close. I reported to Lt. Colonel Arthur Marlow, an expert internist and hematologist, a quiet and dignified man, even-handed and direct. He inspired the medical staff by setting the highest standards of medical competence.

"Among my other duties, I organized and conducted a medical refresher course for a small group of regular Army officers who had served in the field. To make the seminars currently relevant, and to supplement the hospital's medical library, I assembled reprints of recent publications from leaders in academic medicine. I went on ward rounds with other doctors and also reviewed the results of some of their examinations of patients.

"I enjoyed my stay at Ashford, especially the friendly and relaxed atmosphere and the many pleasant social gatherings at the Officer's Club. I played golf a few times, but was no more avid about the game then than now. My wife, Irene, and our little daughter, Elsa, joined me, and we made many friends."

Irene Galdston remembers their day-to-day life in White Sulphur Springs:

"We rented four rooms of the upper floor of a very large house near the hospital. A niece and nephew of the owners each had a room on that floor also. A grand staircase led to that level from the first floor. The house sat high atop a knoll, and was surrounded by beautiful and fragrant lilac bushes. There were very long outdoor stairs leading up the hill to the house. The view was magnificient, but climbing the stairs with our daughter and bags of groceries could be daunting.

"Three of the rooms were spacious and sunny. The kitchen, however, was converted from a former 'trunk room,' and had only a cabinet or two and a small oven, and was without running water. The only source of water was the bathroom, down a long hallway. Friends on their way home from Mississippi once stopped for dinner with us. Thanks to food rationing, the only main course available at the market was goose. We spent hours afterwards cleaning up from that fatty meal, making numerous trips to and from the bathroom for water. It wasn't any fun — we didn't have any detergents then — but looking back it seems hilarious.

"The house was owned by Mr. and Mrs. Basil Ballard and his wife. They were wonderful to us, and we developed a warm friendship. Their five-year-old daughter, Norma Lee, was not very happy with the way her parents doted on our baby girl, and who could blame her? Basil Ballard had been the meat cutter at the hotel before the war and continued in the job when the Army took over. His wife, Maude, had operated the Greenbrier's gift shop. We kept in touch after the war, and twenty years later, their daughter sent us an invitation to her wedding.

"White Sulphur Springs was a pleasant little town, and its citizens were helpful and friendly to Army personnel. But sometimes it was hard to find things. I think there was a general store, but for something like shoes for Elsa, I had to take a bus (we didn't have a car — indeed neither of us knew how to drive) to Covington, Virginia, which was bigger and had more stores.

"One day at our market checkout, I heard some people talking about what would happen when the Army left town. Would the C&O Railway buy back the hotel? Would they again enjoy the benefit of having such a famous resort so near? There was a real concern. It wasn't really long until the Army began to shut down the hospital, and stopped subsidizing our off-base quarters. We moved from the Ballard's to an elegant suite in the hospital.

"Bingo parties with substantial prizes were held to deplete the big balance in the Officer's Club treasury. I won candy and a Longine wristwatch. Big sales also were held to empty the commissary. I bought several boxes of spices and, in my enthusiasm, two enormous tins of strawberry jam. We haven't been back, but we hear from friends who have, and they say the hotel's still lovely. It would be fun to see it again."

Eddy D. Palmer, from Montclair, New Jersey, earned his M.D. degree at the University of Rochester. He joined Ashford's gastroenterology unit in 1946, and still credits his chief, Dr. Robert Hollands, with teaching him many useful medical procedures and philosophies. Dr. Palmer recalls:

"For me, a very special pleasure was the small trout stream which meandered through the hotel property. I made good use of it, but I never took home a catch to eat — they all went back into the stream. Another fun thing I remember

First Lt. Eddy Palmer, M.D., and his wife, Jeanne, with their ten-day old baby, Hannah, in front of their rented house on Mill Hill Drive, White Sulphur Springs.

was that just before the hospital closed, we were told that all the booze left in the Officer's Club would be thrown out if we didn't drink it up. You can guess what we did.

"My wife and I remember White Sulphur Springs as the coldest place we ever lived. We rented a little house down the road from the hospital. It was just one room with a woodstove in the center. It was fun but it certainly wasn't warm. It had the grand-sounding address of 325 Mill Hill Drive — but the 'drive' was a muddy dirt road. We were living there when our first child, Hannah, was born at Ashford on April 17, 1946. She was delivered by my colleague, Captain Ed Banner.

"Closing Ashford was really very sad. My tropical diseases patients were all transferred to Walter Reed Army Hospital, in Washington, D.C., and I soon followed them there. They and I both missed the unique spirit of Ashford General Hospital. There'll never be another like it."

PFC ROY H THOMPSON
13 JULY 73
WARD 601 ASHFORD GENERAL
HOSPITAL
WHITE SULPHUR SPRING L, W VA.

ROBERT FLAVIN JONES
SKETCHED UNDER THE

4

Nurses, Therapists, and Dieticians

The first contingent of thirteen U.S. Army nurses came to Ashford General Hospital from Fort Knox, Kentucky, before the conversion from hotel to hospital was complete. They found, in startling contrast to the somber atmosphere of most hospitals, brightly colored bedspreads and draperies, expensively-tiled bathrooms, and rich furnishings. Though such luxurious touches soon would be replaced by standard government issue, that feeling of living and working in a world-class resort would never leave these first arrivals.

Within a year, the number of nurses would swell to eighty. Assigned to wards, clinics, and operating rooms, most were on duty eight hours a day, five and a half days a week, and served a month of night duty every four to six months. The cottages surrounding the hospital, many with fireplaces and all with spacious verandas, made pleasant living quarters. By late in the war, the nursing staff reached 140 members.

The Chief Nurses were, successively, Capt. Burdette B. Sherer, Capt. Frances Wildonger, Maj. Amelio Leino, Maj.

Madolyn L. Allum, and Lt. Col. Katherine E. Baltz. These officers directed the work of all Ashford nurses in whatever assignments they held.

The Army nursing staff was augmented by civilian nurses, Cadet Nurse Corps student nurses, male orderlies, American Red Cross Nurse's Aides, Red Cross Gray Ladies, and various other volunteers. From mid-1945, some of the Army nurse's work was done by members of the Women's Army Corps hospital companies. This wide range of assistance was needed because of the Army's indecision and delay in establishing the most effectively-sized Army Nurse Corps.

Although physical therapists and dieticians were not part of the Army Nurse Corps, they served worldwide with the Medical Department as commissioned officers, and usually worked side by side with Army nurses. In the course of the war, the Army commissioned approximately 1,600 physical therapists, and an equal number of dieticians. The Army also employed some 900 civilian occupational therapists, who served exclusively in the United States. Despite concentrated recruiting efforts, the Medical Department's need for dieticians and therapists of both kinds was never wholly satisfied. At Ashford General Hospital, as throughout the Army hospital system, the Army nurse was the mainstay of all nursing care.

Esther Alfonso La Barbera was born in Cuba and grew up in Tampa, Florida. She and her younger sister, Mary Teresa, both took nurse's training, and graduated as R.N.s at Good Samaritan Hospital in Cincinnati, Ohio. Esther Alfonso graduated first, passed her "state boards," then accepted employment with the U.S. Public Health Service to work in the Cincinnati area. Later, at the urging of her mother, she joined her sister in entering the Army Nurse

Corps. Together, the two sisters took the six-week indoctrination course at Fort Knox, Kentucky, and were assigned to Ashford General Hospital in November 1942:

"We were the first nurses there, and we saw everything as it developed: the conversion of the hotel into a hospital, the arrival of more and more people, and then the arrival of the first patients. Most of them were from Guadalcanal, but none of them were wounded. They suffered from battle fatigue, and were put into the mental ward. They weren't 'goldbricking.' They were sick.

"Later we began getting casualties from North Africa. Some were airmen who had flown with the British Eighth Army even before the Allied landings in Morocco and Algiers. Many had malaria. By Christmas, all of the wards that were ready for patients were full and more wards were being prepared.

"At one point I spent lots of time with the officer who was in charge of the PX, giving him advice on the special needs of the nurses and other women working at the hospital. He sought such advice so he could order and stock the right things. I told him we needed bobby pins to anchor our caps, soaps and lotions, cosmetics, hair brushes, facial tissues, and those kinds of things. Also, I made sure he knew never to run out of sanitary napkins.

"I was a second lieutenant assigned to the psychiatric unit. We lived four nurses to a cottage and I was in one they said had been used by Secretary of State Cordell Hull. We didn't have that much of a social life. We were too busy. But I did swim in the pool, and go to some of the Saturday evening dances. These were affairs mainly for the doctors and their wives, but the doctors were nice, and danced with the nurses too. I'd held onto a couple of long dresses when I enlisted, and we could wear them off-duty. Almost all the doctors were married, and most lived in town with their wives. There were one or two bachelors, but I didn't especially like them.

Esther Alfonso (r.) and Helen Burch, Army Nurses in civilian attire, winter of 1942-1943, before both went overseas.

"As a result, though it was a 'no-no,' I sometimes had dates with enlisted men from the medical detachment. Most of them were college men waiting for a chance at OCS. It's funny now to remember how discreet we were, sneaking away through the trees at night to some spot called the

Chicken Shack. We'd meet our dates and form a little procession with each of us hanging onto the belt of the one in front of him or her, because it was so dark we couldn't see. The Chicken Shack was a black-owned place where we could eat and drink and maybe dance to a juke box. We bumped into an old Master Sergeant once, and at first I thought he'd turn us in, but he just walked over and told us to never, never go upstairs. I had a hunch what sort of place it was, but I've never really known for sure.

"I reported to the Chief Nurse, a captain, who reported to the commanding officer, Colonel Beck. What a distinguished man he was! He was just a great gentleman and his wife was wonderful, too. I came to know them both well. However, as I didn't play bridge, my chances to 'socialize' were greatly reduced.

"When I arrived at Ashford, many of the professional staff were being prepared to serve in India with the 78th General Hospital there. My sister and I were scheduled to go with them but our orders were changed at the last minute. In May 1943, we were sent to New Orleans for two weeks of training before going overseas. Our destination turned out to be Aruba, the West Indies island where American troops were stationed to protect oil refineries against German U-boat attack.* Many of our men were Puerto Rican, and we were sent there because we spoke Spanish. It all worked out well. While there, I met my husband-to-be, a lieutenant colonel in the Air Force. Looking back, the months I spent in White Sulphur Springs were some of the most exciting of my life. I wouldn't trade them for anything."

---

* The Dutch islands of Aruba and Curacao produced half a million barrels of gasoline and oil derivatives daily. A German U-boat shelled an Aruba shore refinery on February 16, 1942, and further attacks were expected.

Helen Burch Dietrichson finished her nurse's training in 1941, and joined the Army Nurse Corps in October 1942. She was at Ashford with the two Alfonso sisters:

"I had a wonderful time at Ashford, serving with Esther and her sister. We were so young and carefree. It was a very happy time in our lives. We weren't used to so much luxury. We lived in 'Cordell Hull's' cottage with the same original furnishings, and daily maid service provided by a woman who lived in town. At that time they were still modifying the hotel rooms and suites, making them more like barracks and sometimes squeezing eight beds into a room where there had been only two. But it was more efficient that way, and the patients weren't really crowded.

"There was organ music in the lobby, the food was good, and we were enjoying our work, which fortunately hadn't reached the demanding level it would later. As much as we liked it there, however, most of us feared the war might end with us still in the West Virginia hills.

"I also remember the Chicken Shack, but I think we went by cab and met our dates there. Some of us rode on the horse trails up Kate's Mountain. We didn't ride well, but we all tried. Other nurses took up golf, but even with the free equipment and lessons provided, I couldn't get interested. For many of us, Ashford offered so much we weren't used to that we didn't know how to take advantage of it all.

"Our first patients were casualties from North Africa. Among them were numerous men who accidentally had received bad yellow fever shots and as a result had developed a form of hepatitis. They were so badly jaundiced and nauseated they required special and unusual medication. It was like a cereal, and the odor was so horrible I wanted to throw up myself. Getting them to swallow it wasn't easy.

Army Nurse Helen Burch with group of
unidentified patients, Summer 1943.

"In the beginning, enlisted men and officers shared the same rooms because the officer's ward wasn't ready yet. About the time it opened, we started getting combat wounded, and I was transferred to the new ward. I was there until spring, when I was reassigned to a hospital near Plymouth, England."

As many as half of all the Army nurses who served at Ashford also may have served abroad, either before or after tours of duty there. Nurses in the war theaters performed many daily feats of heroism. Over 1,600 nurses were awarded medals for service under fire, and sixteen lost their lives as a result of enemy action. Five hospital ships and a general hospital were named after Army nurses killed in the conflict.

Mildred A. Smith was from Radcliff, Kentucky, not far from Fort Knox, and was interviewed in 1987:*

> The 15th of November, we went to Ashford General Hospital in White Sulphur Springs, West Virginia. That's the old Greenbrier Hotel. It's still the Greenbrier Hotel, a real fancy hotel that is nestled in the mountains. . . .
>
> The first [casualties] we got arrived Christmas Day of '42 from North Africa. They arrived by train that morning. . . . I was on night duty and there was just a little bit of snow and I looked out and the walking wounded were walking up the drive. The others were being brought in by ambulance. They arrived at 6:30 a.m. Whenever we had a group of patients arrive from overseas, we stayed on 'til all the patients were admitted. If we were on night duty, we stayed and helped the day people or vice versa for those who came in at night. That was a standing order. The patients were fed breakfast and we admitted them all. I was working orthopedics at the time, and the first ones that came into the area were all patients who had been in plane crashes. They had a lot of broken legs and broken arms and other injuries. I think that was our first realization that there really was a war going on. This was a 2,000, almost 2,500 bed hospital. It was full all the time with casualties.

* Colonel Smith was interviewed February 10, 1987, by Major Cindy Gurney, Army Nurse Corps Historian, as a part of the U.S. Army Nurse Corps Oral History Program. Such histories are available at the Center of Military History, Washington, DC.

I was just glad we had some place they could come to and I was glad that the hospital looked beautiful for Christmas Day. The patients were just glowing. We were all the same age, you know, and they were so glad to get off the ship they'd been on for so long. That was before they flew them back home, you know. They'd been on the ship, some of them, for two or three weeks and they were so glad to get to a place where they could settle down and get on the phone, call home and talk to their families. I just felt so pleased that I was a little peg in the wheel, to do my part.

It was real funny because we all got off about 11:30 a.m. and we usually worked seven to seven, twelve hours' duty. I could hardly wait to get back on duty that night to see the ones I admitted, how they were doing and how comfortable they were. When we all went on that night you'd have thought that we'd known each other for years . . . They rolled into their nurse's station to say, "Hey, did you get any sleep? Did we keep you up?" You know, those things. I can remember so well that one of them had a father who was a florist in Chicago. On New Year's Day our whole ward was full of flowers. He had told his father [that we nurses loved flowers] and all the nurses' stations had roses.
. . .

The Duke and Duchess of Windsor visited Ashford in October 1943, touring the entire hospital and its grounds, as well as the prisoner of war camp. Both were familiar with The Greenbrier, and indeed the Duke had stayed there while he was still Prince of Wales (he and his party occupying the entire third floor).* A bedridden patient with whom the Duchess spoke gave her a belt he'd just made. The Duke promptly claimed it and put it around his waist. Presumably, the Duke later returned it to his wife. The former

* The Duchess of Windsor (nee Wallis Warfield) honeymooned at the resort with her first husband, E. Winfield Spencer, in 1916. The Duke first visited The Greenbrier in 1919.

King of England was much impressed with Ashford and told *The Ashford News*:

> When I drove up the drive with Colonel Beck, I thought I was driving to the famous Greenbrier and not to a hospital where hundreds of boys are staying recovering from their wounds . . . I have visited several American hospitals. They are all giving fine treatment, but this hospital not only does that but it has retained its great recreational facilities and its beauty.

Ann Clark Miller reported to Ashford, her first duty station after winning her commission as a Hospital Dietician: "I arrived just before Thanksgiving, 1943. Two months later I was sent to Fort Knox, Kentucky to study food preparation in the field, a requisite for overseas assignment. I came

Lt. Ann Miller (r.), Hospital Dietician, and Lt. Ruth Brillhart, Physical Therapist, in front of the "Tansas E Cottage," January 1944.

back to Ashford fourteen days later only to find orders for immediate transfer to join a group of doctors and nurses in Palm Springs, California. They were there preparing to ship overseas as the 81st General Hospital. I left Ashford to join them the same day.

"I don't really remember that much about Ashford, except for living in the `Tansas E Cottage' with three other girls, all of whom went overseas shortly after I did. I was sent to the European theater, and they were assigned to a hospital ship bound, I think, for the South Pacific. Fran Wright and Dot Bradley were Physical Therapists. Mary Alice Alburn was a Hospital Dietician like myself. We were all commissioned as second lieutenants.

"I swam in the beautiful indoor swimming pool and met the Greenbrier's famous swim coach, Charles Norelius. He was an older man who had been a member of the Swedish Olympic Team that competed in Athens in 1906. I'm lucky enough to own a copy of his book, *Swimming.* I loved the water and used the pool every chance I had."

Various stories about the hospital's Dietetic Department appeared in *The Ashford News.* By mid-1943, Ashford's "mess department" served meals to nearly 2,000 patients and up to 1,000 post personnel and civilian employees every day. Most patients had surprisingly hearty appetites: they gained an average of fifteen pounds a man, consuming huge quantities of milk, butter, eggs, fruits and fresh vegetables.

The department's standard practice was to buy these products from local farmers and dairymen. Produce from Ashford's own half-acre "Victory Garden" planted and tended by patients in the reconditioning program was used as well. At first, some mess sergeants may have questioned the strict procedures set up by hospital dieticians, but in time those dieticians made all the decisions concerning food, ranging from how it was cooked and served to how leftovers were discarded. Jokes about the quality of "hospital food" were virtually non-existent.

Arbetta Kashimura Hepfer grew up at Onset, Massachusetts, and graduated from Boston University's Sargent College of Health and Physical Education (now the Sargent College of Allied Health Professions). Answering the Army's call for women with B.S. degrees in physical education, she took a one-year post-graduate course in Physical Therapy at the Walter Reed Army Hospital in Washington, DC. After six months training, and a six-month apprenticeship, she was commissioned a Physical Therapist (PT) in the U.S. Army:

"In the early months of 1944, I was assigned to the Physical Therapy Department at Ashford. Captain Carl Levenson, M.D., was my immediate commanding officer. Our work was demanding, but we did a lot of fun things, especially swimming in the great indoor pool. And, because the Greenbrier's pastry chef had gone to work for the Army, what wonderful food we had!

"I lived in one of the cottages (which I found again years later when my husband and I celebrated our 25th anniversary at the hotel). By the middle of 1944, just after D-Day, we started getting lots of patients back from Europe, and free time was very limited.

"Anne Mashey and Frances Wright were other PTs with me at Ashford. At that time, there weren't many commissioned PTs and we were all females.* Those of us who completed the Army course at Walter Reed were scattered all over the country as well as overseas. Ashford was a sort of VIP place, and was visited for rest and relaxation by many of the top generals. FDR's friend and advisor Harry Hopkins was treated in our PT unit, though why, I don't know.

* The Army used enlisted men as "physical reconditioning instructors" and commissioned male personnel as "physical reconditioning officers," but did not begin commissioning male physical therapists until 1955.

"There was an Army POW camp nearby. Most of the captives had been members of the elite German *Afrika Korps*. We joked among ourselves that it still took three of them to move one chair.

"I met and married Penrod G. Hepfer, M.D. after he came into Ashford's Medical Corps 'pool' prior to assignment overseas. We were married in the hospital chapel on May 15, 1944, by post chaplain, Lieutenant Colonel Robert Clarke.

The "Alabama" cottages were the most remote from the hospital and housed many of Ashford's Physical Therapists (Cummins Photo, courtesy Rosemary Romeyn Dent).

"We didn't have that long together at Ashford. My husband was soon in France where he won a Silver Star serving with the 14th Armored Division. I joined the 140th General Hospital, and by late summer was sent to England not knowing that I was pregnant. Upon that discovery, I was flown home to Mitchel Field, Long Island, and left the service in December 1944."

The Ashford News recorded many marriages at the hospital, the first of them taking place March 7, 1943, when medical detachment Staff Sgt. Earl Verham and Miss Betty Jo Holman were united by hospital chaplain Lt. Col. Oscar W. Reynolds. After their short honeymoon, the sergeant returned to his hospital duties and the bride resumed work in Washington, D.C. Some weddings involving either Ashford patients or staff were performed in local churches, and at least one marriage took place with the groom still bedridden in his room, the bride and chaplain at his side.

The chapel at Ashford was a fairly small room with rows of individual chairs rather than pews. Space was reserved up front for men in wheel chairs. Potted palm trees and fresh flowers surrounded the altar, and contributed to the quiet and dignified atmosphere. A small piano was set to the side. Altar vestments, crosses, crucifixes, hymnals, and scriptures were provided from hospital funds.

Helen McEneany Tabery took her nurse's training and earned her R.N. in Cincinnati, Ohio. Then she enlisted in the Army Nurse Corps in November 1944, in her home town of Columbus, Ohio. After her training at Fort Knox, she was assigned to Ashford in February 1945 and took charge of the orthopedic ward the following month.

"The ward consisted of ninety-six patients and a recovery room for those who went to surgery. Every day, six to nine of our patients had operations for various degrees of bone injury. Our staff numbered three surgeons, six registered nurses, ten to twelve Cadet Corps student nurses, and four corpsmen from the medical detachment. Early- and mid-1945 was a busy time for us, with much pain, and much joy, too, because it was then that I met a patient, Stanley Tabery, who would be my future husband.

"Stage and screen stars visited frequently. Among them were Al Jolson, Walter Pidgeon, Esther Williams, Jean Arthur, Jane Withers, and Signe Hasso. We also were honored by General and Mrs. Eisenhower. The general saw and talked with every patient, asking where they'd fought, and where they'd been hit. I've spent thirty-five years in nursing, and I still have many fond memories of my time at Ashford."

Nurses volunteering for the Army Nurse Corps — like doctors volunteering for the Medical Corps — needed training on how the Army did things. The first training centers were opened in mid-1943 at Fort Devens, Massachusetts; Fort Sam Houston, Texas; and Camp McCoy, Wisconsin. There, nurses were taught the Army's medical, surgical and pyschiatric techniques, and about preventive medicine and ward management. In case they went overseas, they also were taught how to set up tents, dig foxholes, and purify water. New training centers such as that at Fort Benjamin Harrison, in Indianapolis, Indiana, were created as needed.

Many young Red Cross volunteers who served as Nurse's Aides also received Army training, though of a different sort than the new Army nurses received. In early 1944 those at Ashford General began taking an eighty-hour course designed to allow them to perform certain nursing tasks. A "capping" ceremony for the first twenty-member graduating class was attended by the Superintendent of the Army Nurse Corps, Colonel Florence A. Blanchfield,* who told the young women how "impressed and inspired" she was by the good work they were doing.

* Blanchfield was born in Shepherdstown, West Virginia, and, among many other awards, received the State of West Virginia Distinguished Service Medal in 1963.

Othelia Dempsey Tillette grew up in Ansted, West Virginia, and earned her R.N. from Mountain State Memorial Hospital in Charleston. She joined the Army Nurse Corps in 1942, and was stationed at Camp Breckenridge, Kentucky, where she met, and later married, Lt. James L. Tillette. Just before she was to go to North Africa, the Army discovered she was pregnant and discharged her. She returned to Charleston to have her son, but in 1945, when the Army badly needed more nurses, she and her friend, Elizabeth Cole Board, took positions as civilian nurses at Ashford:

"The U.S. soldiers were some of the finest patients a nurse would ever want to care for. It was a privilege and honor to live at Ashford and work there with such wonderful boys. Elizabeth and I were especially happy to serve because both our husbands were overseas — mine in the Army, hers in the Air Force. I worked in the Officer's and Dermatology Wards.

"Though some of the ambulatory patients said they didn't think there was enough to do at Ashford, I really enjoyed my four-month tour there. Elizabeth and I had the cottage once occupied by the Duke and Duchess of Windsor, our meals were wonderful, and our pay was terrific: $350 a month plus room and board. And all that free recreation — swimming, movies, bingo games, billiards, volley ball, tennis, and so forth.

"My mother took care of my son while I was at Ashford, and I would go home by bus each weekend to be with them. We had to furnish our own uniforms. We did our own laundry and ironing and could get most of the things we needed at the commissary or downtown.

"The German POWs who took ill were admitted to the hospital, and were generally good patients. Most were very young, some perhaps only 14 or 15 years old. President

Roosevelt died in Warm Springs, Georgia, while I was at Ashford, and after the announcment, the POWs were returned to their stockade. They seemed glad to return to work the next day. Being stuck in the enclosure, I suppose, was terrible compared to being at the hospital. The stockade was located right along U.S. 60, and MPs were on duty there around-the-clock. Once a friend and I were out driving and parked near the prison. In only minutes, they challenged us with a high-powered searchlight."

Civilian nurse Othelia Tillette in front of the cottage she shared with her nurse friend Elizabeth Board.

Guards at the prisoner of war stockade were understandably concerned about cars parking near the camp. They knew that one prisoner already had escaped from a 40-man work detail cutting timber some ten miles west of the camp. By 1945, most POWs only thought of going home, not of escaping, but some of the camp guards had just been returned from combat in Europe, and had nervous trigger fingers.

Elizabeth Cole Board also from Ansted, West Virginia, and also a Mountain State Memorial Hospital graduate, was never an Army nurse like her friend Othelia Tillette. She'd been a Charleston pediatrician's nurse before accepting civilian employment at Ashford:

"Though Othelia and I shared a Tansas Row cottage, we had very different jobs at Ashford. I worked in orthopedics most of the time. The men were appreciative and co-

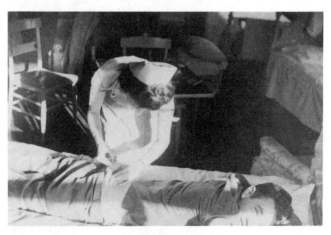

Receiving a short of penicillin (courtesy Clinton Beuscher).

operative, but many were bedridden, some were confined to wheel chairs, and some were pretty depressed over their loss of limbs. Sulpha drugs and penicillin, given every three or four hours, were the main infection-fighting drugs. We also gave penicillin through plastic tubes directly into areas under casts where there were bone and tissue injuries. I later worked in the Officer's Ward, where most of the patients were ambulatory, and didn't require as much care. A big part of our nursing job was to encourage the men to be as active as possible.

The Officer's Ward, better known in peacetime as the "Virginia Wing" (Cummins Photo, courtesy Dr. Charles Magner).

"Everything of a physical nature at the Greenbrier had been kept much the same — the main dining room, the comfortable chairs in the lobby area, the organ room, and so on. Many of the maids, elevator operators, and other hotel employees had been retained. A few were disturbed when they felt that Army personnel were abusing things, but they still remained pleasant."

Prior to the war, The Greenbrier's well-known pipe organ had provided guests with a steady source of entertainment. Early in 1942, the organist was dismissed and the fine old Moeller organ remained silent until 1943, when an Army organist took over its keyboards. From that time, quality musical programs were played daily.

Also located in the organ room was a large Stromberg-Carlson phonograph on which symphony concerts were played daily from 1:00 P.M. to 2:00 P.M. Those who liked popular music could play their favorite records each noon-time except on Sundays. Tunes with a fast beat such as Glenn Miller's "In the Mood," "Kalamazoo," "A String of Pearls," and "The Jersey Bounce," inspired impromptu "jam sessions," where staff and patients jitterbugged to those and other current hits.

Listening to the Stromberg-Carlson (courtesy The Greenbrier).

Ellen McNabb Bates was born and raised in Auburn, Indiana. She took her nurse's training at Saint Joseph's Hospital in Fort Wayne, and worked in its surgery unit after becoming a registered nurse. She joined the Army Nurse Corps in March 1945, and after six weeks at Fort Knox, she was assigned to Ashford as a nurse in the Orthopedics Department:

"When we'd completed our standard indoctrination training at Fort Knox, it was absolutely anyone's guess as to
where we'd be sent. We were called together one morning,
and told that a lucky few were headed for White Sulphur
Springs. My close friend, Kathleen McNamara, was in that
class with me — we'd trained and enlisted together — and
by good fortune we both were sent to West Virginia. The
train arrived in the morning and we had breakfast in the

Army Nurse
Ellen McNabb
looking just as
glamorous as
any recruiting
poster. Here
she wears a
Fifth Service
C o m m a n d
shoulder patch.

dining room. Everything seemed just as plush as when the
hospital had been a resort. I went into orthopedics, but after a month was transferred and trained as an anesthetist.

It was all clinical, on-the-job training provided by Major William H. Galvin who was the hospital's chief anesthesiologist. I became responsible for giving sodium pentathol, nitrous oxide and oxygen, and, once in a while, ether. I also monitored patient blood pressure, pulse, and other vital signs. The doctors administered all spinal injections — numerous because we dealt with so many foot and leg wounds.

"I didn't socialize all that much. Nobody I knew had a car, and going out with an enlisted man was a sure way to be sent overseas. I did see a number of free movies in the hospital. The generals sat in cushioned seats up front, other officers behind them, and then the enlisted men in the back. Really, it was hard for me to feel comfortable. I was a civilian at heart, and if I left the hospital grounds, I had to give and return salutes and worry about protocol.

"Being sports-minded, I spent most of my free time playing the three beautiful golf courses that were available for us. They even had left-handed clubs for me. Another nurse, Mary Black, was the best and I don't know how she put up with me. We all went bowling a lot downtown, not in any league, just whenever we had time and could get a lane. The place only had eight lanes, and two were reserved for duck pins.

"When summer came, the nurses had a softball team and I was the pitcher. I was written up once in *The Ashford News*. We had an extra-inning game going between our nurses' team and the cadet nurses' team — they were mere civilians while we were the 'Real McCoy,' or so we thought. The score was tied going into the bottom of the tenth, when we scored a run to win, 13 to 12. I was both the winning pitcher and the best batter, hitting safely in five of six at-bats.

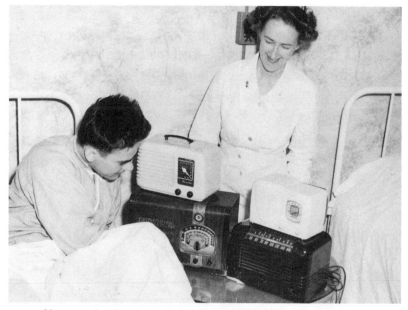

Nurse and patient trying to decide which of four radios donated by West Virginians sound the best (courtesy The Greenbrier).

"The swimming pool was another favorite of mine. They had a former Olympian, Charles Norelius, as an instructor, and he tried to teach me diving. I came up with more black and blue marks on my legs! It was a tremendous privilege to be able to use that pool. My mom and pop and sisters came to visit me once. They were much impressed with the pool and with all the other things about Ashford. As the hospital was closing down in mid-1946, I asked for my discharge. I've never said much about my military service, mainly because I was only in for just over a year, and so many nurses had served overseas under such demanding circumstances, that I couldn't compare to them."

The women at Ashford — nurses, cadet nurses, civil service employees, physical therapists, and, later, WACs — enjoyed sport as much as the men. League softball started in April 1945, when a Cadet Nurses team beat an Army Nurses team, 14 to 7. Non-league competition at volleyball and basketball was held on "girls nights" at the gym. Ashford All-Star female teams also played such challengers as the Greenbrier College for Women, usually trouncing them easily.

Second Lt. Mildred Wood, Physical Therapist, served at Ashford in 1945-1946.

Mildred Wood, from Williamsport, Pennsylvania, received her degree in physical education from the East Stroudsburg State Teachers College. She was teaching at a high school in New York state when she decided to enroll in a twelve-month Army training course in physical therapy. The course was given at Ashford General Hospital. At the end of that training, she was commissioned a second lieutenant:

"Twenty of us were accepted for the training, but one girl failed her physical, and so there were only nineteen in our class. For the first six months, we were physical therapist aides, and through the final six months, physical therapist apprentices. The first part was the hardest: we had classes from 8:00 A.M. to noon, then from 1:00 P.M. until 5:00 P.M. every day, including Saturday. We spent Sundays getting set for Mondays again. We had a crash course in anatomy — the names and the functions of all the bones and muscles had to be learned — and other subjects such as massage, whirlpool bathing, electrotherapy, the use of 'heat cabinets,' and the testing and evaluation of a patient's progress. Gradually we were introduced to real patients and began getting practical experience. During the second six months, most of our work was in the physical therapy clinic, and we had more time to ourselves.

"I wasn't commissioned with the rest of my class, because I couldn't meet the Army's minimum weight standard. But I had been stuffing myself, and next day my parents drove me — by then heavy enough to qualify — to Washington where Adjutant General James Ulio pinned on my bars. I rejoined my classmates and we all spent six weeks in basic training at Fort Devens, Massachusetts. By then the war was over.

"I was sent back to Ashford as my first real Army posting. It was probably early October, 1945 when I arrived, and I stayed until the hospital closed about eight months later. There were six of us physical therapists. The others were captains, so I was 'low man on the totem pole.' All our work was hands-on. We didn't have other people doing the hard work for us and, though the war was over, there were still lots of men arriving from overseas needing therapy.

Patients with arm and leg injuries receiving hydrotherapy (whirl-pool bath) treatments before exercising (courtesy Mildred Wood).

Patients in the therapeutic gym of the Physical Therapy Clinic performing supervised exercises (courtesy Mildred Wood).

"Patients sought physical therapy for a variety of problems. Our most frequent visitors seemed to be men with peripheral nerve injuries. Treating nerve damage was one of Ashford's specialities, along with treating cardiovascular and brain injuries. We eventually made whole again a fellow who had broken his neck diving into a foxhole. Other men had more common problems, such as bursitis or arthritis. Some were simply exhausted. We didn't do any work downstairs in the swimming pool. That therapy was given by the people in the reconditioning program.

"Our physical therapy clinic was on the third floor of the bath house. Below us, the big swimming pool was on the first floor, and the occupational therapy rooms were on the second floor. A lot of the Greenbrier's original bathing equipment remained. We didn't use the sulphur water baths for therapy although in our training we were made familiar with how they worked. But we did use the long tubs, with ordinary heated water that bubbled up from beneath, somewhat like a sauna. A few men would fall asleep in those baths. We made sure they didn't stay in too long.

"When Ashford closed, I was reassigned to the Tilton General Hospital at Fort Dix, New Jersey, then later to the Walter Reed Army Hospital in Washington, D.C. Though scheduled for release in 1950, I was 'frozen' in place when the Korean War began. I left service in 1954, but stayed in the reserve and retired as a colonel in 1980. I've yet to see the Greenbrier again, but because of all the fond memories it holds for me, I certainly want to."

From its start-up on August 10, 1944, Ashford's Physical Therapy training course asked a lot of its candidates: more than 1200 hours of instruction in twenty-one subjects and a reasonable skill in each type of treatment used. The school was directed by Capt. Carl Levenson, M.D., and classes were taught by Capt. Agnes Snyder, PT, and medical staff members. Mildred Wood's class graduated on August 9, 1945. A second and last class graduated in March 1946.

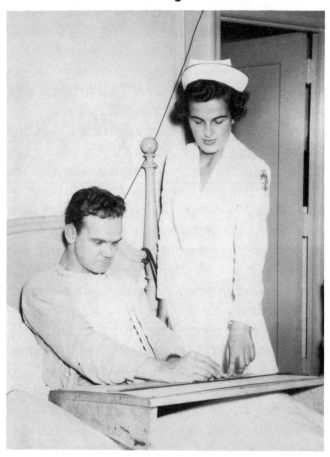

Occupational therapist Rosemary Romeyn showing a patient how to use a drafting board and a T-square.

Rosemary ("Posey") Romeyn Dent was a civilian occupational therapist at Ashford and the second floor clinic was where she spent much time teaching patients a variety of arts, crafts, and other skills. Born in Meadowbrook, Pennsylvania, she had taken a degree in occupational therapy from the University of Pennsylvania in 1943. She'd then worked as a therapist at a state mental hospital until she started her duties at Ashford in September 1944:

"My time at the hospital was glorious. Under the general direction of Mildred Bond, who headed Ashford's OT section, I supervised an occupational therapy program for about

Occupational Therapy Department, Rosemary Romeyn back row center.

two hundred and fifty bedridden men and thirty-five paraplegics. That gave me a chance to learn about neurovascular injuries and rehabilitation techniques, and I was paid $2,644.80 per annum, which I thought was a fortune."

Ashford's Occupational Therapy Department officially opened its doors in November 1944, with Capt. Carl Levenson, M.D., as its head, and 2nd Lt. Mildred Bond as chief therapist. Occupational therapy had by then evolved into a program in which wounded men themselves completed the work of doctors and surgeons through exercises that reduced the effects of residual damage. Patients learned to control their healing muscles by doing exercises on shoulder wheels, wrist bars, and finger ladders.

By weaving place mats, cutting jigsaw puzzles, modeling clay figures, or completing many similar projects, patients also overcame certain psychological barriers that might have caused them to "favor" their wounds and impede their healing. Until 1944, Red Cross Arts and Skills Corps volunteers had served as the Army's *de facto* occupational therapists, and they had done axcellent work without the Army's direction. After the Army established a planned program, classes were gradually added that would actually help patients develop skills useful in civilian life. Among them were carpentry, car mechanics, metalworking, and typing. Eventually, men could choose from among dozens of such activities, all of them valuable sources of mental and physical stimulation.

Ann Wright Lawson, born at Kanawha Falls, West Virginia, completed her first two and a half years of nurse's training at the Charleston General Hospital, and her final six months as a Cadet Nurse at Ashford General Hospital. She graduated in March 1946, and was eligible for an immediate commission in the Army Nurse Corps:

"At Ashford, we weren't considered part of the Army. Our only obligation for everything given to us — tuition, room and board, uniforms, and a modest monthly stipend — was to remain in essential nursing for the duration of the war. We were not required to enlist in the Army Nurse Corps, though obviously the Army hoped we would. When I en-

rolled in the program, I could have gone to a hospital operated by any of the services. I chose Ashford (and the Army)
because I knew the Greenbrier. Three or four of us from
Charleston went there together. I believe that mine was the
second of only two classes to graduate at Ashford.

Ashford's first graduating class of Cadet Nurses paraded for General Mark
Clark, summer 1945 (courtesy The Greenbrier).

"We lived in the Lester Building Annex, halfway between
the main hospital building and the Casino. Each morning,
bright and early, we did calisthentics in the parking lot. We
took close order drill there as well. Of course, the main part
of our student nurse's training was taking care of patients
and we worked with them all the time. We did other things
with them, too, like shopping or bowling. Sometimes we
even played tennis with those who were able to play. The
medical training we got, which was the most important thing,
was every bit as good as that we received at Charleston
General Hospital. We observed a 9 P.M. curfew, but we still
had time for some entertainment in the evening, in my case
mostly bowling. I went home on weekends a lot in some-

body else's car and often took some of my girl friends with me. We took patients home for weekends, too. After graduation I returned to Charleston General for a year, then went to Detroit for thirty more years of nursing."

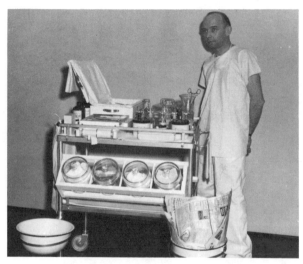

Orderly and rolling cart equipped with everything needed to change dressings (courtesy J.W. Benjamin, Jr.).

The United States Cadet Nurse Corps was established July 1, 1943. Before ending in 1948, this U.S. Public Health Service program had helped to train 124,065 graduate nurses, many of whom had spent their last terms in an Army hospital. They were not members of the armed services, and the Cadet Nurse Corps pledge was a statement of good intentions rather than a legal contract:

In consideration of the training, payments, and other benefits which are provided me as a member of the United States Cadet Nurse Corps, I agree that I will be available for military or other federal, governmental, or essential civilian nursing services for the duration of the present war.

Katherine Owens Pollard, originally from Greene, New York, had completed two and a half years at the Hahnemann Hospital School of Nursing in Philadelphia, Pennsylvania, before she joined the Cadet Nurses Corps. She was one of a group of thirty-five student nurses recruited from various hospitals in the area to be assigned to Ashford. Another twenty-five Cadets were sent there from the Pittsburgh area. Starting in March, 1945, all sixty would be trained together as a single unit, in surroundings they soon called "Ashford Tech":

"Like all the others in the Cadet Nurses Corps, we agreed to stay in active nursing for the duration of the war, and when we signed up we could request assignment either to the Army, the Navy, the Veterans Administration, the Bureau of Indian Affairs, or the Public Health Service. I was lucky and got my first choice — the Army — and White Sulphur Springs was a terrific plus.

"We left Philly on a cold, dismal March night, and woke up the next morning near Clifton Forge, Virginia. We saw that the mountains were all covered with redbud and dogwood, and when we got to Ashford the tulip and daffodil beds were all in blossom. Our trip was an overnight journey from winter to spring.

"We were met by two Army nurses, Captain Elizabeth D. Simon, and Second Lieutenant Bernice H. Kress. They directed us for the six months we were there. I shared a room in the Lester Building annex with Pat Ford, who also had been studying at the University of Pennsylvania, and two other girls from the Pittsburgh area — Lorraine Niles who'd been in the Duquesne University School of Nursing, and Helen Nicolette who'd been in the St. John's School of Nursing. When we arrived, the nursing staff was badly shorthanded, and remained that way for our first three months.

Then came a detachment of medical WACs to help out. Our patients were mostly suffering vascular or neurological injuries. Because such injuries rarely would be seen in civilian practice, our doctors had to 'write the book,' developing sound treatments as they went along. Two unusual

Capt. Elizabeth D. Simon, head of the Cadet Nurses at Ashford (courtesy Pat Ford).

specialists worked with us: one was a photographer who took pictures of the new surgical procedures and, at intervals afterwards, the results for the patients. The other specialist was a draftsman-artist who made detailed sketches of the operations. These drawings and photos were used by the surgeons to teach the techniques to others.

"Most of our patients were from the Italian campaign, from Bastogne and the Rhine offensive, with only a few from the South Pacific. Most came by hospital ship from England to New York, and were classified by type of wound and sent to appropriate hospitals from there. I can't begin to say how wonderful the men were. Some 5,000 patients came and went while I was at Ashford and I can remember only one who was unpleasant.

"General Eisenhower was there for the premier of 'The Story of G.I. Joe.' The movie's combat scenes were so realistic that they disturbed some of the patients, and gave them bad nightmares. If we had to give them penicillin shots after they'd gone to asleep, we learned to awaken them by gently touching their ankles. If we didn't, they might just come up swinging.

"Even though many of our patients were in pretty bad shape, they were extremely courageous, and seldom lost their sense of humor. There was one ward of hemiplegics and paraplegics. They were the saddest and yet the most wonderful. I had that ward on V-E Day and when I came on duty they insisted I have a drink with them. They were enjoying some moonshine brought in by a ward attendant. Since it looked like only water, I thought 'why not?' When I swallowed some, and nearly lost a lung coughing, the four guys in the room had hysterics. I've thought of those men many times over the years, wondering whatever happened to them.

"The Cadets had a certain amount of military training. We were taught close order drill, and we proved pretty good at it. Occasionally, we were shown Army films. The one about loading trucks really threw us. After that we couldn't help wondering, 'what next?' We'd been told to leave all of our civilian clothes behind, but playing various games in a hot uniform wasn't much fun, so I wrote home asking mom and dad to send me some sports clothing.

"During my six months there, many of the top Army generals and their wives came to White Sulphur Springs for some rest and relaxation. Besides Ike and Mamie — whose sister and parents also came — I saw Mark Clark, Jonathan

Wainwright, Omar Bradley, and many others. They were all so nice to the boys, usually removing all insignia of rank so they needn't be saluted. I fell in love with General Eisenhower when he held a door open for me, and it never wore off.

"A few of us even had a theatrical career at Ashford. Along with some patients and duty personnel, we put on a play. We never made it to Broadway, but it was fun. We were surprised and pleased to be asked to repeat our show for the patients at Woodrow Wilson General Hospital in Staunton, Virginia. We did an afternoon and evening performance. Woodrow Wilson was a standard cantonment-type Army hospital, and after spending a day there, we realized how lucky we were to be at good old 'Ashford Tech'!"

The "standard cantonment-type hospital" was similar to those built overseas: of the simplest possible construction, with sixty to seventy one-story buildings all interconnected with enclosed heated hallways. Compared with Ashford, they would seem barren and depressing. All but three of the twenty-six such hospitals built in the United States were transferred to the Veterans Administration after the war ended.

The medical photographer remembered by Katherine Pollard was probably T/5 Joseph T. Jackson. He and anatomical artist T/5 Vincent Destro assembled the "Ashford Exhibit" for an Association of Military Surgeons conference in New York City in 1944. With only a high school drawing course as previous experience, Destro had enrolled in the art classes taught at the hospital by Mrs. Anne Post who'd once operated her own art studio in New York. After Destro had shown an unusual aptitude, he was given an office and installed as a "medical artist." He made the detailed drawings used in exhibitions and medical journals from the sketches he made while viewing surgical procedures in the Ashford operating rooms.

T/5 Vincent Destro was the hospital's anatomical artist *par excellence* (courtesy J.W. Benjamin, Jr.).

Pat Patterson grew up in the Philadelphia area, joined the Cadet Nurses Corps in early 1945. She opted for the Army, despite her father's objections (he had been a Navy man). Like her friend, Katherine Owens, she had completed her first thirty months of training at Hahnemann Hospital School of Nursing, and felt that with a war on, everyone should do their part:

"At Ashford we mostly were given practical experience. We'd finished most of our classroom work before we got there. We were moved around through the different wards, so that we'd see a whole range of problems. I spent a lot of time in the eye, ear, nose, and throat clinic located on the hospital's lower level, where the luxury shops had been before the war. We handled lots of sinusitis and tonsil cases. We had plenty of just plain 'floor duty,' too, mostly tending patients who had head wounds or nerve damage. We weren't assigned duty in the operating rooms, but I noticed and was especially amazed at how quickly they got the men up and around after surgery.

Cadet Nurses (l. to r.) Kay Owens, Pat Patterson, and Beth Hoffman at the volleyball net (courtesy Pat Patterson Ford.

"When we were on duty, we wore the student nurse uniforms from the schools we had attended before, so everyone knew where everyone else was from. We paid for those uniforms ourselves. We were, however, given dress uniforms: white blouses, gray skirts, and gray jackets that were trimmed with red piping. We wore these uniforms to drill, stand inspection, and for any official activity. We also wore them to dances.

"Captain Simon was wonderful, a fine Army nurse, well-liked by all the Cadets. She saw to it that we behaved ourselves, and administered such discipline as might be needed. About all she ever did, actually, was to suspend our weekend leave privileges or something like that. We weren't really in the Army, so she couldn't be too tough.

"We didn't go into town very often, since there was so much to do right at the hospital. I learned about 'Rum and Coca Colas' at the Officer's Club and I saw lots of movies in the theater. What a place that hospital was! I'd never seen one like it before. Every patient was treated like royalty, and even the German prisoners had it made.

"We worked hard and there wasn't always time for much else, but when there was, we enjoyed playing volleyball in the gym and we had a healthy rivalry with the Army nurses. I met my husband-to-be at Ashford. I was with another fellow, trying to learn to play golf, when I hit him with a ball. He was a paratrooper with the 101st Airborne Division and was wounded at Bastogne, Belgium, during the Battle of the Bulge, December 1944.

"We weren't supposed to see enlisted men but many of us did. Sometimes, we'd double-date with somebody who had a car, and go to the Chicken Shack for drinks and snacks. You needed a car. A taxi cost too much. Toward the end of my training, my fiancé brought his own car down from Maryland and we went around as we pleased. We were married in 1946. Two years later, we returned to see the Greenbrier and play some golf, but we stayed at a motel in town because the resort was too expensive."

Ruby Lewis Watlington was one of eight children born on a tobacco farm in Rock Springs, Virginia. After completing high school and working for several years, she entered and later graduated from the University of Virginia School of Nursing. In December 1942, she enlisted in the Army Nurse Corps, and following various stateside assignments, served in England, France, and Belgium, coming back to the States in November 1945:

"Returning from a forty-five day leave, I was assigned to Ashford General Hospital, a great place to work — and to play! With long months of overseas duty behind me, and the war over, I did all the things there were to do. I hiked in the mountains, had my one and only go at golf, enjoyed good dinners in the Officer's Club, and relaxed and wrote dozens of letters. The PX had the best butterscotch sundaes I've ever tasted, before or since. Sometimes, during dinner hour I'd just write letters and listen to the music in the lobby. I mostly worked the 3 P.M. to 11 P.M. shift, and could take a train to Danville on weekends."

Most of Ashford's nurses, both civilian and Army, lived in what had been The Greenbrier's cottage rows. The cottages, all dating from before the Civil War, were one-story wooden buildings, and the names of many rows reflected the resort's "Southern" heritage, among them Alabama, Florida, Georgia, Louisiana, Paradise, South Carolina, and Tansas.* Most of these cottages were within a crisp five-minute walk of the main buildings of the hospital or — when there was less rush — a lovely ten-minute stroll under the trees. At one point, the U.S. Corps of Engineers wanted to

---

* The six cottges of Tansas Row received their unusual name because the owners of the first two were from Tensas Parish in northern Louisiana. How "Tensas" became "Tansas" is unclear.

level the cottages, and build new housing in their stead. Col. Beck's emphatic "no!" ended that threat, and it was never renewed.

Some of Ashford's 126 Army Nurses in May 1946, Bess Armstrong is sitting middle row, center.

Bess Armstrong Hatfield was a Canadian R.N. who joined the Nurse Corps, and served overseas before coming to Ashford: "In 1942, I was working as a nurse in the United Church Missionary Hospital in Hearst, Ontario. A unit of American soldiers arrived there, presumably on their way to guard the Hudson Bay coast. After talking with them, I decided to join the Nurse Corps and by 1943 I was in Europe. Because I could speak some French, I was assigned to the hospital at Rennes, France. On V-E Day I met an American officer who told me if I ever got a chance I should ask for duty at Ashford. Well, I got the chance, asked for the assignment, and arrived there on December 1, 1945.

"Believe me, it was great. I had a room of my own in one of the cottages, second from the main gate, and I worked in the surgical ward. By the way, I married that officer I met on V-E Day. He turned out to be from Hanover, West Virginia, and knew the hotel very well."

Army Nurse Bess Armstrong with her husband-to-be, Capt. Kennie E. Hatfield, the often-mentioned Howard's Creek in the background.

Most West Virginians were aware of The Greenbrier, because it was then the Mountain State's chief claim to fame. Below the national average in income, education, and health care, West Virginia was often perceived outside the state as being populated by barefoot hillbillies with rifles in one hand and jugs of "white lightning" in the other. Many West Virginians who resented this view of their state— including some who had never even seen The Greenbrier — took great pride in the resort, and its very different image.

Edith E. Beardsley grew up in Garretsville, Ohio, and took her RN training at City Hospital in Cleveland. After Army Nurse Corps basic training at Fort Benjamin Harrison, she was assigned to duty at Ashford on April 15, 1944:

"I reported with the expectation of something very different ahead. I was assigned a room in the Hawley House, which was really luxurious, indeed. The hospital certainly didn't look like a hospital! I especially remember the lovely dining room and the beautiful chandeliers.

Edith Beardsley served in Germany after the war.

"I'll never forget the first time I saw a group of wounded men arrive. They were right off the ship from Europe, having come up from Newport News, Virginia, on a hospital train. I had just come on duty. We worked twelve-hour shifts to feed and make them comfortable. They seemed so young, and I forgot that I was about the same age.

"Later, just before the war ended, I served in the Pacific, and later still in Europe. I ended up with thirty-five years of service, and retired as a colonel. Joining the Army was the best move I could have made. I met so many wonderful people, including those at Ashford."

Laura Kelly grew up a few blocks from the capital building in Providence, Rhode Island, and joined the Army Nurse Corps in 1930 at the age of twenty-one. Between 1930 and 1932, she served at the Walter Reed Army Hospital and later at several other hospitals. Just before coming to Ashford, she had been in France, and on V-E Day she was in Paris, just as her father had been on Armistice Day in 1918:

"At Ashford I was in charge of the area where communicable and intestinal diseases were treated, and also responsible for certain ambulatory cardiovascular patients. At first, my quarters were in the main building. But there were so many roaches that I complained, and they moved me into one of the cottages. I'm sorry to say that it just wasn't that clean. Some nurses actually reported brushing roaches off the patients' dressings before they could change them. You see, the place had been a hotel and the cleanliness levels probably had never been kept up to Army standards. It was necessary to remove the wallpaper and the rugs to clear up the problem. In all other ways, Ashford was very adequate.

"We had patients from all of the active theaters of war, a little bit of everything. Most of our gunshot wounds were from the Battle of the Bulge and we did a lot of 'shunting' operations — taking out bad sections of veins or arteries, and tying the ends into good veins and arteries. We got a continuing stream of intestinal problems from the Pacific, various kinds of parasitical diseases. Once V-J Day came, however, we really weren't that busy. During the last six months — I was there until the hospital closed — we were probably overstaffed, if anything.

"I didn't drive, and even if I could have, the Army didn't allow nurses to keep cars. But train service was readily available, and I rode over to Virginia on several weekends to visit a patient I'd taken care of at Walter Reed. I was not at Ashford long enough, really, to get involved in its many social activities. I nevertheless enjoyed each minute of my twenty-five years of Army nursing, including my time at Ashford."

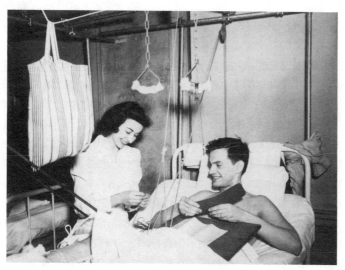

Army Nurse Pat McCormick with unidentified patient (courtesy John Arbogast).

White Sulphur Springs was on the C&O mainline midway between Washington, D.C. and Cincinnati. *The Sportsman, The George Washington,* and *The Fast Flying Virginian* were three of the C&O's best-known passenger trains and during the war they served an ever-increasing number of riders stopping in White Sulphur Springs.

Kathleen McNamara finished her nurse's training in 1944 at St. Joseph Hospital in Fort Wayne, Indiana, and joined the Army Nurse Corps early the next year. After basic training at Fort Knox, she went straight to Ashford General Hospital. Like so many other nurses, she was deeply impressed by its elegance, and by being assigned to live in a cottage where the rich and famous had once vacationed:

"The recreational facilities were terrific. Though I wasn't a golfer then, I enjoyed walking along the famous courses. I played volleyball and tennis, and I swam in the magnificient indoor pool. We also went on picnics when someone had a car. We had time for several overnight train trips to Washington for a day of sightseeing.

"After the war ended, we had lots of generals who came to Ashford for rest and relaxation. There was even a 'general's row' of seats in the front of the hospital theater. Most famous was General Eisenhower, who brought 'Mamie' with him. One of my friends was assigned to special night duty outside his suite. Hers was a very short assignment — when General Eisenhower found her, he sent her away, saying the injured needed her more.

"Night duty was a particularly challenging time. Penicillin was still new, and was administered by injections every few hours. A WAC would go with me and hold a flashlight as we tried not to wake the patients. A team of orderlies would then turn each patient as gently and as quietly as possible. Many patients woke up anyway, so night rounds were a time of quiet chats and just 'listening.' I remember one man who was worried about his parents' first visit. We solved his 'first time together' problem by having me meet them, then join the three of them for dinner. I wish some of the other patient's problems could have been solved that easily.

"There was one young dental officer whose arm had been so severely injured that he couldn't practice dentistry again. His career had ended before it ever began. We had many long talks about his options, one of which was enrollment in law school. I've always hoped that he did that, and had a long and successful 'second' career.

First Lt. Kathleen McNamara had this portrait made when she was home on leave from Ashford.

"The majority of my patients were in the spinal injury ward. That was difficult but rewarding. Though many patients were even younger than I, some were not expected to fulfill their normal life expectancies (fortunately, new treatments based on continuing Army and Veterans Administration research brought new hope for many). We were assigned to the same group of patients for daily care, and soon learned each patient's emotional needs.

"That worked well for those we cared for regularly, but not always so well when we relieved other nurses. Some patients pulled pranks, while others became angry with the 'sub.' We understood how frustrated and bitter many were, and we tried our best to calm them. We needed and had a strong supportive staff to help us all — patients and ourselves alike — get past some difficult days and nights. That support came from corpsmen and WACs and from caring physicians who fully explained what was ahead for each patient.

"After the war ended, and Ashford, along with many other hospitals, was soon to be closed, a number of our spinal cord injury patients were sent to the VA hospital in Richmond. I was one of the nurses to go with them on the hospital train. It was heartbreaking, going from the beauty of the buildings and grounds of the old Greenbrier, to that somewhat stark VA hospital. Many of the men realized they might have to spend their remaining lives there. I don't know who shed the most tears: the patients during that train ride to Richmond, or we nurses on the train ride back to White Sulphur Springs."

5

Medical Detachment Personnel, WACS, and MPs

The first thirty-four enlisted men of the 3590th Service Unit (the medical detachment) arrived in White Sulphur Springs on a cold, foggy morning in October 1942. Trained for hospital service, these men and the hundreds to follow, would provide most of the hospital's skilled and unskilled labor.

Those first arrivals could hardly believe their good luck. They enjoyed fine meals in the hotel dining room, where they were served by polite waiters and waitresses. Their rooms in the McKenzie and West Virginia buildings (formerly reserved for various Greenbrier employees) were kept immaculate by housekeepers. They knew it couldn't last, and it didn't. Soon, they began eating cafeteria-style, cleaning their own rooms, and working to help the hospital become functional.

Medical detachment men worked in the wards, the finance and personnel offices, the post office, the kitchens — wherever they were needed. In late 1943, the detachment totaled 525 enlisted men and was headed by 1st Sgt.

Roscoe H. Ahl. First Lt. Lewis A. McAmis, the post Provost Marshal, commanded the unit, and later was succeeded by Capt. Willard A. Bryant and then by1st Lt. Earl D. Harkness. All three men were Medical Administration Corps officers trained in handling the day-to-day management of the hospital.

Members of the Women's Army Corps (WACs) were late arrivals on the Ashford scene. The first, Sgt. Agnes L. Hicks, came in September 1943, and, like the many other individuals and small groups to follow, Hicks was quartered separately from but "attached" to the 3590th medical detachment. Brand new WAC barracks were built in March 1945 and more WACs arrived each week.

In May, *The Ashford News* reported that there were fifty-six WACs working at the hospital, most of them West Virginians. In June, when the number reached 200, the 52nd and 53rd WAC Hospital Companies were activated, with Capt. Patricia Reed commanding the 52nd, and 1st Lt. Elizabeth McRee, the 53rd. Colonel Oveta Culp Hobby, the Women's Army Corps commander, came to Ashford to inspect the new units.

Many of the WACs at Ashford had joined the service as the result of a recruiting campaign aimed at attracting 50,000 medical technicians to replace medical detachment men who were being assigned to combat units. Especially needed were women who after graduation from a Medical Technician's School could serve as technicians in orthopedic clinics and various testing laboratories. Though the recruiting drive fell short of its goal, the WACs who completed the training performed very well. None did the heavier work of male orderlies: they were considered to lack the stamina for long hours of pushing heavily loaded food and linen carts, lifting large objects, and scrubbing wards and corridors.

Ashford also had two groups of military police: the 412th Guard Company, which maintained law and order and protected the security of the hospital and its grounds, and the 486st Military Police Escort Company, which guarded German POWs. As a part of hospital security, the 412th enforced parking and traffic regulations, assured the good behavior of Army personnel in White Sulphur Springs, operated the hospital's guardhouse, and supervised all the civilian guards who were hired to help them.

William H. McDonald, a native of Central City, Kentucky, was twenty-one years old when he was sworn into the Army at Fort Benjamin Harrison, Indiana, in late 1942. Private McDonald was given no basic training, but was sent directly to Ashford's medical detachment:

"About all the training I got at Ashford was the day our sergeant hiked us up Kate's Mountain on some dirt road, and at the top hollered out 'dismissed.' I guess he wanted to see if we could find our own way down again.

"One of my first jobs was working in a crew that cleaned out the swimming pool. They said it had cost a million dollars to build it. We were down in there scrubbing all that fancy tile with long-handled brushes and some kind of a cleaner. I don't remember how long it took, but it was hard work.

"Since I could type, I later was assigned to the admissions and dispositions office to do paperwork. For some months I worked the night shift, typing disposition reports for every person in the hospital, including everyone coming, going, or just changing rooms or wards. My report was reproduced, and a copy put in every in-basket around the place. It was like a daily census. The nice part about the night shift was that I was excused from inspection next morning and could sleep as long as I wanted.

"The medical detachment's barracks were across the railroad tracks from the main gate to the hospital. We walked back and forth to the hospital across a foot bridge over the C&O tracks. I stopped on the bridge lots of times to watch the long coal trains struggling up the grade toward Covington, Virginia. Sometimes I wondered if they'd actually make it. A lot of trains went by at night. They might wake you up at first but after a while you wouldn't notice.

"I really enjoyed my stay there. It was a beautiful place. I went downtown now and then, and went to a certain restaurant with a juke box where a lot of soldiers went to have a few beers. I didn't drink but I liked the companionship. Once in a while I'd hop an evening train over to Covington, and walk around just sightseeing, or go to a movie or something until it was time to catch another train back. I guess I had some girl friends over there, too.

"I was at Ashford for about eight months or so, then they transferred me to the Huntington, West Virginia induction center. There I was taken off limited duty — I had a bad eye — and so became eligible to go overseas. I then took basic training at Camp Ellis, Illinois, and went to France with the 202nd General Hospital. Through good luck, I drew 'detached' service at the Hotel Victor Hugo in Paris for a number of months and altogether I was overseas for sixteen months.

"I've revisited the Greenbrier a number of times, walking around and through the lobby and all, but that place is too rich for my blood. I couldn't afford to stay there."

Teresa D'Elia Jones grew up in Brooklyn, and partly to avoid a marriage arranged by old-fashioned Italian parents, joined the WAC in January 1944. Even though he later was intensely proud of her decision, at first her father was so angry that he wouldn't speak to his twenty-six-year-old daughter. After completing basic training at Fort Oglethorpe, Georgia, D'Elia was sent to the 18th WAC Hospital Company, then in Kentucky:

"Before we came to Ashford, my company had been stationed at Nichols General Hospital in Louisville. Though our new post was beautiful, our new barracks were just like WAC barracks anywhere: rows of single cots down each side of two floors; small, corner rooms for higher-ranking noncoms; and showers and other bathroom facilties on the ground floor. We shared a small day room with two other WAC hospital companies, the 52nd and the 53rd. Captain Iola Solem was our commander and we all loved her.

Tech. Sgt. Teresa D'Elia and statuary near the Kate's Mountain NCO Club, early 1946.

"My first assignment was to the Quartermaster unit in the stable area just off the airport road. I handled the linen exchange mostly, checking the incoming shipments and making the necessary disbursements. I walked to work — it took ten minutes or so — through a tunnel under the road, returning at noon for lunch in the main hospital building. Later on, I became our unit supply sergeant working in a QM storeroom in the barracks area. Just before the hospital shut down, I was given the job of walking through the wards and listing all the furniture and fixtures the Army would leave behind.

"My group of girls didn't date much, and didn't get involved in the various sports things that were available. I liked to bowl, but the lanes were in town, and we didn't go into town much except to shop for cosmetics, or for things we couldn't get at the hospital commissary. I grew up in a poor family where golf and tennis were considered luxuries for the rich, and I knew nothing about them. Off-duty, we enjoyed lounging around in pajamas in the day room, or our barracks, drinking wine and playing five-card stud with a three-cent limit.

"One of the things I especially remember about Ashford is that there were so many high-ranking officers. Where I'd previously been stationed, a full colonel was like a god, the absolute tops, and rare at that. But at Ashford, full colonels were a dime a dozen, nearly as common as 'second looeys' elsewhere. Three- and four-star generals weren't unusual, either. The golf courses were crowded with them.

"Our company First Sergeant, 'Sevie' Severson, was good about always giving the girls a helping hand. She used to keep a big gallon jug of change on her desk. Anybody that came up short before payday could borrow from it, then pay back the 'loan' at their leisure. Sevie helped me get several weekend passes to go home to Brooklyn, and that's how I learned that my father had forgiven me for joining the WACs. Each time I returned to duty, he'd slip ten dollars into my uniform pocket. That was when ten dollars was a lot of money, too. It really made me feel rich.

The 18th WAC Hospital Company, Sgt. D'Elia kneeling fourth from right.

"At Ashford when the weather was good, my friends and I liked to climb Kate's Mountain and have a picnic. We'd take a six-pack of beer and some sandwiches and have a ball, just three or four of us girls. We didn't go in the lodge, which was the NCO Club, but just in front there was a funny statue of some wood nymphs, and we'd pose and act silly there while someone took a snapshot. I liked Ashford, and before we left I won the Army Commendation Medal. General Beck pinned it on my blouse himself."

Looking across the C&O tracks and U.S. Route 60 to the WAC barracks in foreground and the hospital buildings beyond (courtesy The Greenbrier).

Kate's Mountain* was a great place for hikers and riders to observe nature. Though few visitors may have known it, most of the West Virginia's 1,600 flowering plants could be seen there, as could deer, rabbits, foxes, squirrels, and an odd black bear. To be avoided were copperheads and rattlesnakes and lots of poison ivy, ticks, and "chiggers."

The Kate's Mountain Noncommissioned Officer's (NCO) Club was widely considered the most beautiful in the country. A part of the Greenbrier estate bought by the Army, Kate's Mountain Lodge was designated an NCO Club in early 1943 by Col. Beck, whose only proviso was that it be well-used. Built of logs, the rustic one-story structure dated back to 1918 and always had been a popular rest stop for The Greenbrier's guests who liked to ride the Kate's Mountain trails. Besides plenty of tables and chairs, the lodge

*Named for Kate Carpenter who, *circa* 1750, fled there with her baby in her arms when Indians attacked her Howard's Creek homesite. According to legend, mother and daughter hid in a hollow log while the Indians vainly searched all about them.

boasted a kitchen, a bar, and a dance floor. White Sulphur Springs could be glimpsed through the trees hundreds of feet below.

Though the lodge's capacity was restricted, there was ample room for various entertainments. Detachment dances were held regularly and featured such home-grown musical groups as the "Greenbrier Gully Jumpers," the "Greenbrier Joy Makers," and the "Kanawha Mountaineers." Indi

Full house for one of the many comdies and dramas presented by Charleston's popular troupe of "Kanawha Players" (courtesy The Greenbrier).

viduals and groups came and sang, danced, juggled, told jokes, and performed skits. The "Kanawha Players," an amateur theater group from Charleston, did scenes from "Junior Miss," a play they had presented at the hospital.

Melvin R. Schwing was born and raised in New Martinsville, West Virginia, and was inducted into the Army at Fort Hayes in Columbus, Ohio. From there, he was sent immediately to White Sulphur Springs:

"We had a bit of basic training there, with Sergeant Willis H. Rust giving us some close order drill on the platform of the C&O station. We also took some hikes in the mountains, but that was the extent of it. There were never any guns or anything like that.

Post Office staff, 1944, commanding officer Capt. Charles E. Hurst, center, and Pvt. Melvin Schwing at his left side (Cummins Photo).

"We were quartered in brick barracks, which weren't regular Army barracks, but more like dormitories. I understand they had been used before the war to house hotel employees. I was in the 'West Virginia' Building. The other was the 'McKenzie Building.' Both were together just south of the C&O tracks. We were at the base of Kate's Mountain and the road up to the NCO Club went right past the barracks.

"My main job at Ashford was as a clerk in the post office. It was basically an eight-to-five job in a crowded cubbyhole about the size of an average living room. Those patients who could, came down for their mail, but the orderlies delivered it to the bedridden. Mine was an undemanding job, and I got home fairly regularly on weekends.

"When others learned that I'd played trumpet in my high school band, I was invited to join a dance band that was just starting up. My friends insisted that I send for my horn, so I did. All the band activities were strictly voluntary and on our own time. We played for some local dances in White Sulphur Springs, at the Lewisburg Country Club, and at a bond rally in Covington, Virginia. Most of our work, however, was right at Ashford, at dances for the patients and the staff. We were called 'The Generals.'

The Ashford Generals played for live audiences at the hospital as well as in adjoining towns; pianist Marion Gibbons at far left (courtesy The Greenbrier).

"We had some really great guys in that group. The original leader of the band was Jack Stern, another trumpet player, and he was followed by Clifton Burmeister who later became Dean of the School of Music at the University of Wisconsin. Some of the others were Bob Hiatt, Sal Toro, Jim Pohl, and Marion Gibbons, who was our pianist. 'Gibby' also gave the noonday organ concerts. He was a great musician.

"For something else to keep me busy, I became the 3590th Medical Detachment bugler. Sergeant John Huber had the job, but didn't really want it, and happily turned it over to me with the assurance that I'd be promoted. The job was pretty easy: all I had to play was reveille, first call, and taps, with everything repeated twice — once facing one barracks, then again facing the other. I got nothing at all for this (including no stripes) except the 'privilege' of getting up before everyone else did.

"Once we were told that someone very famous soon would be visiting the hospital, but not who it would be. A week or so later, as I was talking with friends in the hall outside the post office, here comes General Eisenhower walking down the corridor. As 'Ike' neared them, the German POWs working there snapped to attention and their boots cracked together like rifle shots. They stood like ramrods until he'd passed, while most of the American soldiers just threw him a casual 'highball.'

"Something I've never forgotten was watching a trainload of wounded men arrive at the White Sulphur Springs C&O station. They were coming in from Europe and they looked so young — like they were mostly eighteen or nineteen. Many had been badly hurt, but I've never seen a happier bunch in my life! They had survived the war.

"I wasn't all that outgoing, and didn't date much. I saw a few movies, and I tried my hand at golf. I wasn't much of a golfer, but I played some on the nine-hole course set aside for beginners. I also used the swimming pool a lot. Playing in the dance band was the big thing for me."

Almost every issue of *The Ashford News* seemed to announce another dance, with music to be provided by "The Generals." There were "March of Dimes" dances, "Sweetheart Dances" on Valentine's Day, "New Year's Eve" dances, V-E and V-J Day "Victory Balls," a "Leap Year Ball," a "President's Ball," and many others. Depending on the number of people expected to attend, dances were held either in the main ballroom or in the gymnasium.

Often the dances raised money for charity by charging the men a dime to vote for a "Queen of the Ball." In addition to the many dances for enlisted personnel — both patients and staff — dances were held quite often at the Officer's Club. "The Generals" played the latest dance music and were always much in demand.

Hospital patients and staff also enjoyed the music of many visiting civilian bands. The eighty-piece Charleston High School Band played one week, followed the next week by the fifty-piece Barboursville High School Band. The bedridden patients, unable to go outside to watch the drum majorettes do their snappy routines, weren't left out. The girls later split up and visited as many of the men as possible in their rooms.

Louise McCoy Turos was originally from Syracuse, New York. At Ashford using her married name at that time, she was 1st Sergeant Louise ("Sevie") Severson of the 18th WAC Hospital Company. After earning a diploma at the National Recreation School, she had taught dancing and drama for the Syracuse Recreation Commission, and later held a similar civil service position in Florida. She enlisted in the WAC in December 1942, at age thirty:

"Being First Sergeant was like being a mother for the company. I'd discuss any major problem that arose with Captain Solem, then take appropriate action. If it was only a minor thing I'd handle it myself. What stands out in my memory are the friendships. I guess I must have been a halfway decent First Sergeant. At Christmas I still get about seventy-five cards from former WAC friends.

WAC 1st Sgt. Louise "Sevie" Severson later served at the U.S. Military Academy at West Point, New York.

"Our barracks were just south of the main hospital building, across U.S. Route 60 and the C&O tracks from the barracks of the 3590th Medical Detachment. We held a lot of parties in our own day room, but we also spent a lot of off-duty time in the Kate's Mountain NCO Club.

"All the girls were either high school graduates, or had passed the G.E.D. equivalency test, and some had college degrees. Those assigned to the wards all had had medical training. Those assigned to the labs, clinics, and X-ray rooms had received special training. Most of the girls were well treated by the medical staff. Patients liked them a lot because they could kid with them easily. They were like 'the girl next door.'

"I remember a stray dog that wandered into the WAC area and more or less adopted me. I called him 'Chips' and General Beck allowed me to keep him. One day 'Chips' went to visit the hospital on his own. When I went over later, I happened to go into the general's office, and there sat 'Chips' on his desk with the general's big Doberman eyeing him. My arrival probably prevented mayhem. When Ashford closed, 'Chips' went with us to Pratt General Hospital in Coral Gables, Florida."

Sgt. Marriott and his canaries (courtesy J.W. Benjamin, Jr.).

Of the many pets at Ashford, the most unusual may have been the pair of canaries rescued by M/Sgt. Stanley Marriott from a destroyed home in Aachen, Germany. Somehow, he had managed to keep the birds throughout his return to the United States for hospital treatment. When the pair produced three eggs, Sgt. Marriott and his pets were reported in *The Ashford News* and became instant celebrities.

Marion E. Gibbons of Brewster, Ohio, was an accomplished musician when he was inducted at Fort Hayes in March 1943. By coincidence, the hospital's Special Service unit had just asked the Fifth Service Command headquarters for a man able to play Ashford's pipe organ. Gibbons, in the right place at the right time, was assigned immediately:

"When I was drafted I was placed in limited service. I think I arrived at Fort Hayes on a Thursday to take various tests and complete various forms. One of the forms asked recruits to list their talents, hobbies, special training, and so on. Among other things, I said I could play the piano. Only at the last second did I add that I also could play the organ.

"By the following Wednesday I was at the C&O train station in White Sulphur Springs, being met by an MP sergeant. You can imagine my awe-struck feelings crossing the grounds to the main building to report in. I'd never heard of the Greenbrier and had absolutely no idea of its grandeur.

"Inside, I was taken to the Special Services office, where I was introduced to First Lieutenant Robert B. Parker, who was in charge of that group. I remember many of them quite well. Sergeant James H. Shelton edited *The Ashford News*. Corporal Walter Hazeltine, who came to Ashford as a patient, but was kept on when his talents became known, drew the newspaper's cartoons, and later became the ranking noncom in our office and more or less directed everything we did. Corporal Philip Q. Seabrook was the chief projectionist in charge of movies. Private Julian Roberts maintained the patients' room radios, and Private John Baker did whatever needed to be done. Mary Miller, a civilian from Columbus, Ohio, was our secretary.

"There were many more of us, but the names escape me now. We all had special jobs, yet worked together as necessary. Two POWs helped clean the office and performed other chores. Our office took up part of the main ballroom. The remainder was a recreation area, filled with Ping-Pong and card tables. We pushed those aside when the ballroom was used for dances.

"White Sulphur Springs, a nice little town and full of friendly people, was just beyond the main gate. My family visited me several times, staying in one of the small hotels with a restaurant.

"The Special Service men who were single, like myself, lived in the medical detachment barracks. We took our meals in the enlisted men's cafeteria, although enlisted men and officers could socialize if they wished. On evenings when the organ room was quiet, someone might ask me if they could listen to a classical record on the Stromberg-Carlson phonograph, then various nurses and enlisted men would sit around and listen.

"We worked very closely with the Red Cross recreation staff, and spent lots of off-duty time with them. I remember their busy director, Irene Spitz, and Mary Ann Potts, Mary Boggs, and Virginia Lewis.

"Among all these recollections, of course, I best recall the wonderful hours playing the organ. Often while I played, the audience, and even the casual passers-by in the lobby, would sing and whistle along spontaneously. Almost every time that I was about to play I would see a row of guys in wheelchairs waiting for the music to begin.

"I also helped pick the popular records played at noon-time on the Stromberg-Carlson. Although our collection consisted mostly of Army-distributed 'V-discs,'* we main-tained a large library of records that had been donated to

Pfc. Marion Gibbons (far left) helping to sort incoming Christmas presents, 1944 (courtesy The Greenbrier).

by individuals and service clubs all over West Virginia. I also enjoyed acting as a guide and host for visiting USO entertainers and sometimes a Hollywood celebrity. I'd take them here and there, and also to the wards to see bedrid-

* Twelve-inch, double-sided phonograph records produced for the Army's Service Service Division by volunteer artists and distributed worldwide by the millions starting in late 1943.

den patients. I met Irving Berlin and Al Jolson, and played for Esther Williams when she sang a few ballads during her swim show at the pool. I also met bandleader Les Brown and his vocalist, Doris Day. She and I enjoyed a chocolate sundae together in the PX. I played piano in 'The Generals' dance band, and we did various dances, both at and away from the hospital, and sometimes put on performances in the hospital theater. Charleston radio station WCHS taped some of these special shows for rebroadcasting.

"After two years at Ashford, I was transferred to Camp Lee, Virginia, to begin training for overseas. By December 1945, I had got as far as California and was awaiting shipment to the Philippines, when I heard of an Army policy prohibiting men with over twenty-one months of prior service from being sent overseas. I immediately placed a long-distance call to my former Special Service boss, asking whether he could use me again. Within the week I boarded a train headed back to White Sulphur Springs and I stayed there until the hospital closed."

As Ralph Fisk previously explained, when the hospital closed, the Moeller pipe organ was sold to the Presbyterian Church in Ronceverte, West Virginia. In 1993, Marion Gibbons went back to White Sulphur Springs, and while he was there also visited the Ronceverte church. A *Beckley Herald-Register* photographer captured the beaming organist at the keyboard. "I just had to see the Greenbrier, and play that organ one more time," he said.

John M. Kiernan enlisted in the Massachusetts National Guard in 1940, and graduated from Officer Candidate School at Fort Custer, Michigan, three years later. Assigned to the 486th Military Police Escort Company at Camp

Breckinridge, Kentucky, his first task was to escort 1,000 German POWs to the "Camp Ashford" enclosure in late summer 1943. He stayed there about a year. Remaining in service after the war, he retired on April 30, 1962, at Ft. McClellan, Alabama, as Lt. Col. Kiernan:

MPs guarding a pay table (courtesy Virginia Kahoe).

"When I first arrived in White Sulphur Springs, I had a room in the Gillespie home on Main Street. When my wife came, we rented an apartment in town. I divided my time between the camp and the hospital, going around the grounds every day to check on POW work details and going inside to visit the POWs who might be hospitalized for one reason or another. I did not speak German, but many POWs spoke English.

"The prison compound followed the standard Army layout for a thousand men: a certain number of barracks, mess halls, and other buildings, enclosed with double barbed wire fences and watch towers at the corners. Each tower was manned on a 24-hour basis, and the guards had .30 caliber machine guns, and searchlights. The enclosure was right beside the airport.

"Work details were taken back and forth to the hospital in small personnel carriers. While I was there, we didn't have buses or large trucks and it was too far to march them twice a day. A small number of men worked at a logging camp near East Rainelle, which was a town maybe thirty or forty miles west of White Sulphur Springs. They established a branch camp there, and didn't have to commute every day. I visited the camp often and can still picture the tiny, narrow gauge railroad used to haul the logs out.

The Duke of Windsor with MP Officers inspecting the German Prisoner of War camp (courtesy The Greenbrier).

"My wife and I enjoyed some informal socializing. We knew Colonel Beck, who was well liked by all. I didn't play golf at the time, and that was surely a pity, because now I'm an avid golfer."

The last German prisoners of war left Camp Ashford in June 1946, just as the hospital was closing. They had not only performed their assigned duties well but had contributed to the hospital's mission in other ways: they farmed their own vegetable garden, and sometimes shared some surplus with the hospital; fought forest fires; and made contributions to Red Cross drives. The Germans also completed a fine wooden altar started by the Italians, and gave it to the Andrew S. Rowan Memorial Home in Sweet Springs, West Virginia.

Leon Benedict of Cadiz, Ohio, was sent to a quartermaster unit attached to the 3590th Medical Detachment immediately upon being drafted in September 1943. At Ashford, Pvt. Benedict received certain training in handling the wounded:

"Once, coming back disheveled and caked with mud from head to toe after practicing winter litter-bearing techniques, I ran into Colonel Beck. He looked me up and down, almost in shock. 'Isn't this the Medical Corps anymore?' he demanded. Obviously, the Colonel didn't know about the exercises we'd been doing.

"I found out that there's more than anyone might think to getting a badly wounded man onto a litter and then carrying him across rough terrain as combat medics do — often under fire. Thank goodness I never had to do it, though after my Ashford assignment was completed, I did become a medic with the 549th Field Artillery, part of the U.S. 9th Army. Later we served with General Patton's 3rd Army and helped to free the surviving inmates at Dachau — a horrible experience.

"At Ashford, though we were getting trainloads of casualties every day and I assisted in off-loading the litter cases, my principal job was running the paper baler in the basement of the hospital. That was part of the quartermaster unit's job: disposing of all the waste the hospital generated. Although hand-operated, the baler was a big, heavy machine that could turn out 500-pound bales of paper products. Those bales were sold to a Staunton, Virginia salvage company, which sent its trucks to the hospital daily to pick them up.

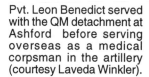

Pvt. Leon Benedict served with the QM detachment at Ashford before serving overseas as a medical corpsman in the artillery (courtesy Laveda Winkler).

"I had a lot of help from four German prisoners of war. I couldn't speak any German, except 'arbeiten,' the word for 'work.' Even so, I never had a problem. The prisoners were dependable men, who worked a steady 8:00 A.M. to 5:00 P.M. day. They would never think of running away.

"Until I left Ashford in April 1944, I lived in one of the brick barracks beyond the railroad tracks. We had reveille and retreat, but I don't remember any other formations. We did some close order drill now and then just so we wouldn't forget how. I went into White Sulphur Springs occasionally, and attended one or two detachment dances. That's how I met and became friends with Laveda Winkler, a volunteer hostess from Charleston. We still exchange Christmas cards.

"I remember there was once a little mountainside forest fire, and we were all called out to fight it. By the time we got there it was well under control. We jokingly called it the 'Battle of Ashford Hills.'"

The Ashford News described, in somewhat florid language, the 'heroism' shown by various personnel in fighting that forest fire (potentially more dangerous than anyone ever admitted):

> Surrounded by more traffic than Kate's Mountain has seen since the invention of the motor car . . . the wind kept high, the flames shot skyward, the smoke billowed, the men fought on and into it . . . The fire was here, then there — it was everywhere — and lungs were filled with smoke. Down into the yawning darkness went out men, many of whom had never seen a forest fire before.

Lowell Shaffer came to Ashford from Ft. Benjamin Harrison, Indiana, in September 1945 and remained there for some time after the hospital closed in mid-1946. His first assignment was to the Officer's Pay Section of the Finance Office, but he asked for a transfer to the MPs when it was certain that Ashford would close:

"I wanted to stay there as long as possible. My transfer was granted, and five of us remained to guard the property until the C&O Railway could take over again. I was there until the autumn of 1946, then went to Pratt General Hospital in Coral Gables, Florida, accepting the previous open invitation from General Beck, who had taken many of his staff there with him in June.

The enlisted men's bar in the Casino (courtesy Erich Steiner).

"I did some wild things at Ashford, such as swiping a case of beer from the NCO Club, trading it for moonshine back in the hills, then returning the moonshine to the NCO Club. On our final day at Ashford, another MP and I decided to shoot the windows out of an abandoned barracks at the prisoner of war stockade. I drew my .45, aimed, and pulled the trigger, and poof! The defective round traveled about ten feet and fell to the ground. That was the only gun I ever fired all the time I was in the Army.

"I feel fortunate to have been posted at Ashford. I golfed a lot, and in the evenings played tenor sax with some other fellows to entertain the patients. I'll be happy to see a book about Ashford. I've always believed that the feelings of the people who were there, whether happy or sad, deserve to be recorded for posterity."

Among the medical detachment men and MP personnel were some fine athletes. Although Ashford's patients participated in such individual noncontact sports as bowling, swimming, and golf, more physically-demanding team games, like basketball and softball, were generally the exclusive province of post personnel. Intramural leagues were formed, and, from among them, players were named to all-star teams that played high school, college, and military academy teams from throughout West Virginia and Virginia.

For example, in the first full basketball season, 1943-1944, an Ashford All-Star team defeated Greenbrier Military School 44-43, Virginia Military Institute 42-35, and the Bluefield All-Stars 49-40. The Ashford team also played the Charleston Boys Club, the Charleston Sport Mart, Woodrow Wilson General Hospital, Nitro High School, the Welch Moose Club, and West Virginia Tech. Additional opponents were added the following two years. The All-Stars didn't win all their games but they did post an overall winning record.

Delphine Marino Szaraz was born and raised in the "Little Italy" neighborhood of Cleveland, Ohio, and joined the WACs in 1944. She was assigned to Ashford in mid-1945 and was a counter clerk in the post office until the hospital closed. One of the eight people needed to keep the mail moving, she was busy six days a week:

"My job was mostly selling stamps and money orders. We also sold insurance for parcels, handled registered letters, and issued war bonds. I didn't sort or distribute incoming mail — other people did those things — but I remember how much letters meant to all the patients. About five years ago, I went back to the Greenbrier with my sister. I had forgotten how beautiful it was."

L. R. JOHNSTON
GENERAL MANAGER

Dear Folks:

This letter is being written on stationery which was formerly used at one of the world's most famous resorts--The Greenbrier Hotel in West Virginia.

In September 1942 the magnificent hotel and cottages were
taken over by the Army and converted into a 2000-bed general
hospital. All of the luxurious furniture and equipment contain-
ed in the building were left intact, and patients are now enjoying them to the fullest extent. Our recreation facilities
are superb. We have an air-conditioned movie theatre which
seats 560 patients. Our dining room is a tremendous room with
expensive and elaborate chandeliers hanging from the ceiling
and we are eating our meals on white tablecloths. In addition,
we have a beautiful tile swimming pool inside the main building, five Har-Tru tennis courts, two 18-hole golf courses, and
about 6000 acres of ground where we can exercise at will and
enjoy mountain scenery which is incomparable. The climate is
ideal, and even on the hottest summer nights we have to sleep
under a blanket. Everything is being done for our comfort and
we are made to feel at home. So even the graciousness for
which the The Greenbrier was famous has not been lost in this
transition from hotel to hospital.

Visitors who come here to see us are received in a spacious lobby beautifully furnished, and I can assure you a
"welcome" sign hangs on the Main Entrance. This is indeed the
"Shangri-La" for sick and wounded soldiers!

I am a patient in Ward No._____.
                         Ashford General Hospital
                         West Virginia.

"America's Most Beautiful All-Year Resort"

Form letter provided to all patients (courtesy William O'Donnell).

Just as they were with soldiers overseas, frequent letters were enormously important to the morale of patients
and post personnel. For those men unable to write, whether
because of injury or a lack of writing skills, printed form
letters and post cards were supplied. The form letter began
"Dear Folks: This letter is being written on stationery that

was formerly used at one of the world's most famous resorts," and ended, "I am a patient in Ward No.__ Ashford
General Hospital, West Virginia."

The form letter was actually the front page of a four-
page color brochure, the two inside pages of which described and depicted various Greenbrier scenes, while on
the back cover there was a map of the hotel and grounds
(see page 15). The message to parents and loved ones
was that the sender-patient was being wonderfully cared
for. Many men wrote home with more details about where
they were than what was being done to them.

The amount of mail coming and going through the
Ashford post office was impressive. A report for the year
ending November 1944 revealed an average of 10,148 letters mailed daily. For the year, there were approximately
7,000 registered letters, and 12,000 insured packages.
Captain Charles Hurst was the hospital postal officer. In
1944 he was in charge of eight to ten men, many of whom
later would be replaced by WACs.

Clarence R. Noble was born near Princeton, West Virginia, was drafted in September 1943, and eventually served
in the 28th Infantry Division in Europe. He was taken prisoner on December 16, 1944, the first day of the Battle of
the Bulge. During the 104 days of his captivity, he acquired
a stomach disorder, and lost sixty-five pounds. After a long
recovery in the United States, he was assigned to Ashford's
medical detachment:

"I was one of the hospital orderlies. I fed the patients,
washed them, dressed them, gave them enemas — the
whole nine yards. I considered myself a male nurse, and I
didn't mind what I had to do. I had seen worse. I had forty

patients in my ward, all of them with serious spinal injuries. I'd take the men who could manage wheelchairs downstairs and over to physical therapy, and so forth.

"I walked to work from our barracks every day at 8:00 A.M. and returned about 6:00 P.M. just like any working guy. As I recall, we had every other weekend off. That's when my wife and I (she moved to White Sulphur Springs while I was there) would jump in my 1936 Ford sedan and head for Princeton, an hour's drive, across U.S. 60 to Lewisburg and then down U.S. 219. I didn't have any trouble getting enough gasoline. We even drove over to Covington to see a movie now and then.

"I didn't take advantage of the USO shows and the golf and tennis and such. My work was hard enough that, come evening, I was tired and all I might do was drop by the Casino for a beer. I enjoyed my work at Ashford, because the men in the wards were great, and I knew I was honestly contributing to their recovery. I'm sorry I didn't stay in touch with them."

Before The Greenbrier became a hospital, the interior of the Casino (or golf clubhouse) was spacious enough, but somewhat austere. In March 1945, to provide a more cheerful ambience for recovering patients, Army personnel using materials at hand did some redecorating. Walls were painted moss green ("bright and restful," said *The Ashford News*), lounge chairs were re-covered in red, white venetian blinds and bright new draperies were added, and an all-white piano was installed. *The Ashford News* wondered "Could Hildegard ask for more?"

Apparently the answer was "yes," since, in September, the Casino was changed again, this time to resemble a sidewalk cafe. A new entertainment policy made Fridays "date nights," with all tables reserved, a floor show, and dancing to live music. Enlisted patients and duty men were required to have dates — no stags allowed. "If no date is available," said *The Ashford News*, "the Date Bureau will supply one." Cold sandwiches, beer, and soft drinks could be purchased at the snack bar. Floor show acts were presented by both amateurs and professionals.

Though United Service Organization (USO) shows with big-name stars were always popular, they were not the only successful theatrical performances at Ashford. Nearly as familiar were the touring, all-Army shows produced by Army Special Service units. Many fine actors and entertainers, after enlisting or being drafted, found themselves serving in such units. Army productions — the best known being Irving Berlin's musical, "This Is The Army" — toured as complete packages, carrying their costumes, make-up, lighting, and sets with them.

The third type of show was that staged entirely by hospital patients, post personnel, and civilian employees. The first of many productions, "Hospital Daze," was staged on January 31, 1945. Such shows, put on by the "Ashford Theater Workshop" were popular because anyone with talent could participate. Really polished, professional performances weren't required. The Red Cross staff scouted the hospital for new acts, and promoted the shows in *The Ashford News* column "Red Cross Jottings."

Russell J. Cole was from New York City. While serving with an antiaircraft unit attached to the 36th Infantry Division near Salerno, Italy, a portion of his left arm was destroyed by shrapnel. His arm was saved, but only after seven months and five operations in the 25th General Hospital in Bizerte, Algiers. He was returned to the U.S. and sent to

Ashford for further neurosurgery:

"It was sometime in March 1944 when we landed at Charleston, South Carolina. We were met by a WAC band. I'd never even seen a WAC before, let alone know they had bands. I was at Stark General Hospital only two days when they put a tag on my litter with the letters, 'WSS.' I asked someone what it meant, and they said, 'Oh, you're headed for a great place, the Ashford General Hospital in White Sulphur Springs, the old Greenbrier Hotel.'

"I had two operations at Ashford, and my arm was restored to about ninety percent efficiency. During my rehabilitation, I met a girl who was a student nurse in a nearby town. After graduating, she came to work at Ashford as a civilian nurse, and we were married. When my treatments at the hospital had been completed, I was offered a chance to stay on as part of the Special Service unit and I took it.

"I began in the reconditioning program, and was a swimming instructor for a while. I got to know the Greenbrier's long-time swim coach and former Olympian, Charles Norelius, who'd coached Johnnie Weismuller, the first movie Tarzan. I worked with many paraplegics — wonderful guys. They'd bring their wheelchairs down a special ramp right into the water. Later, I'd take a bunch to the gym for fifteen or twenty minutes of floor exercises using beach balls and hand weights. I didn't make friends with them because I was afraid it would become too painful.

"Another of my jobs was touring visiting performers around the wards. As an example, when Les Brown and his band came, they split up into small groups and went into the wards and rooms to play requests. Special Services supplied 'portable' pianos that could be rolled along with them. Everyone said that the orchestra leader and his vocalist, Doris Day, were wonderful. I played tennis with her three days straight on number one court — not bad duty!

"Still another of my jobs was running the bicycle repair shop. We had about fifty old, beat-up twenty-eight-inch, single-speed bikes that were used in the reconditioning program. Several POWs worked in the shop fixing flat tires, and broken spokes and such.

"I also got involved with some theatrical shows the Special Services unit helped stage. I had several different parts in some shows written by Marion Hargrove. One was 'Dear Mom,' where a G.I. sits on the edge of the stage and tells the audience about the events of the day at a hospital, while behind him the cast pantomimes them in a series of ten-minute skits. I enjoyed my work at Ashford but once the war ended I wanted out, and I left in November 1945."

Mayhem in Surgery skit from the Ashford Theater Workshop show, "Dear Mom," March 2, 1945 (courtesy Russell Cole).

Sgt. Russell Cole making a pitch at the microphone during the October 1945 "Country Fair" held in the post gymnasium.

Wherever entertainment and recreational opportunities were concerned, the Special Service Office, under Capt. Robert B. Parker, had its finger in nearly every pie: it provided the equipment and the supervision of all sports, booked visiting entertainers and USO shows, coordinated the receipt of gifts from individuals and organizations throughout West Virginia, arranged free transportation for patients attending distant sports and other entertainment events, published *The Ashford News*, and conducted all public relations efforts.

Bertha ("Bert") Vaivoda O'Brien was from Rochester, New York, went to business school there, and worked for a time in the payroll department at Eastman Kodak. She had wanted to be a nurse, but things hadn't worked out as she'd hoped. In January 1945, she was waiting to take a bus when a mail truck stopped for a traffic light right in front of her:

"The side of the truck carried a big sign saying, 'Join the Medical WACs' or words to that effect. 'That sign is meant for me,' I thought. I went to the recruiting office to sign up right away. I liked my job at Kodak, but I felt I was going into

WAC Cpl. Bertha Vaivoda wearing the dress uniform in which the WAC companies paraded for General Eisenhower (courtesy Victoria Vickerman).

work I had always wanted to do. Traveling on the troop train to Fort Oglethorpe, Georgia, was an experience. I liked basic and the medical training we received afterwards. When we finished, we got our T/5 stripes and were given a choice of hospitals. I don't know why I picked Ashford, but it was perfect and I loved it.

"We were trained more or less as nurse's aides, but a little beyond. We did everything to help out the nurses, including giving penicillin shots to patients. Only the RNs could give them narcotics, of course. We also were like 'big sisters' to a lot of the wounded men. I sewed on more hash marks and stripes than I like to remember. We ran errands as well. In West Virginia, or 'West-by-God-Virginia,' as some called it, hard liquor could only be bought in state stores, and seemed overpriced. On paydays we made 'whiskey runs' to Virginia, where we could buy what the boys wanted for a cheaper price. I didn't drive in those days, but accompanied the 'smuggler' on his 'errands of mercy.'

"We did many of the less glamorous jobs, too, like making beds, giving bed baths, emptying bedpans, and serving meals. If someone had a special diet, we made sure he got it. POWs brought up steam carts with the meals from the main kitchen. They also did the KP and kept the kitchen clean. Those that I worked with were plesasant and helpful. Many of the POWs spoke English, so communication was never a problem. I was always friendly with them, and one even made a ring for me. I hope he didn't think my wearing it meant we were engaged!

"I once rode up in an elevator with General Eisenhower. He was wearing shorts, evidently having just finished a round of golf. Gallantly, he insisted that I enter the elevator before him.

"We frequently went to the Casino to drink beer and play the jukebox and to see and be seen. Or we would go to the PX for coffee and also to see and be seen! On the warmer, pleasant evenings, we all might sit around outside on the deck of the Casino, have some beers and just socialize while we gazed at the beautiful mountains in the distance. Hard to believe but some were over 3,000-feet high. The

NCO Club was way up some mountain — and a steep climb. I only went there once, to a Christmas eggnog party. I know I rode in a car with a group, but who my date was I don't recall. Guess it wasn't a very memorable date.

"As far as going into the town of White Sulphur Springs, I didn't much. So many things were always happening around the hospital, there wasn't any need to. One of my

Watching and feeding the swans was a popular relaxation for patients and staff alike (Cummins Photo, courtesy Dr. Joseph Justo).

best WAC friends, Vicky Vitkovsky, and I liked outdoor things best, and they were enough to keep us happy. There was a little lake down by the golf course with a bunch of swans gliding around on it. We'd beg bread from the mess hall, borrow a rowboat, and go out to feed the swans.

"I don't remember standing inspections or doing close order drill at Ashford but we paraded to honor General Eisenhower and General Wainwright when they were there. Incidentally, I never wore the 'Hobby' hat — a high, round, pillbox hat with a bill, which had been designed by our WAC commandant, Colonel Oveta Culp Hobby. They were no longer issued when I was a WAC.

"We had a pinky-beige, button-down-the-front dress we wore on duty. We were issued seven of them, and they easily saw us through a five-or six-day work week. Off duty, we wore whatever we wished. Slacks were popular. I loved Ashford, and was deeply disappointed when it closed."

The third anniversary of the organization of the WAC was celebrated at a May 14, 1945, party and dance arranged by men of the medical detachment for Ashford's WACs. By then, there were 170 WACs at the hospital, with more coming each week. Corporal Jeanne Houston, whose "What's Actually Cooking" (later "WACs Works") columns appeared in *The Ashford News*, thought the evening was ideal — "cool enough for tropical uniforms and warm enough for that Off Duty dress to satisfy that well known woman's desire to be a little different."

Victoria Vitkovsky was a nineteen-year-old from Rochester who joined the WAC at the same time as her friend "Bert" Vaivoda. An entire group entrained from Rochester on March 6, 1945, stopping in New York City to be feted by the Second Service Command headquarters before continuing on to Fort Oglethorpe:

"We all were specifically recruited for medical technician training and, after basic and other training classes, were assigned to various army hospitals. We were automatically promoted to corporal and in time both Bert and I became sergeants. Later, I was commissioned a Second Lieutenant and subsequently was promoted to First Lieutenant while serving in China and Japan.

Victoria Vitkovsky (l.) and Bertha O'Brien play shuffleboard with an unidentified soldier; the famous Presidential Cottage is in the left background (courtesy Victoria Vitkovsky Vickerman).

"From Georgia, I went directly to Ashford and there, based on various aptitude tests, was selected to learn how to use an electroencephalogram, a device that measured brain waves as a means of detecting brain injuries. At that time, there were only a few of the machines in the country. The EEG not only pinpointed the locations of brain damage, but detected epilepsy patterns as well.

"Although it may not have been designated as a stateside evacuation hospital, in essence Ashford was just that. The patients coming into our department had what appeared to be battlefield dressings. Many of the head wounds were ghastly. It took a lot of intestinal fortitude for me to clean those wounds before applying the electrical leads. If the man's scalp wasn't clean enough to make a good contact, the brain wave pattern wouldn't register and the procedure would have to be repeated. I'm really amazed some lived.

"Colonel Beck was the commanding officer, and was, to quote some of the G.I. personnel, a real 'pistol.' A regular guy, he still could lay into someone like a drill sergeant. Some of the patients bought an old used hearse, and drove it all around the hospital grounds. Colonel Beck confronted those men and ordered them in his best drill-sergeant voice, 'Get that god-damned hearse off my hospital grounds!'

"We worked hard, but had a generous amount of free time to take advantage of all the recreational facilities provided. We had marvelous food, as many of the German POWs were good cooks. They even made powdered eggs look and taste good.

WAC Cpl. Victoria Vitkovsky did KP alongside German prisoners of war assigned to the hospital kitchen.

"Some of the Germans were assigned to grounds maintenance. I remember when I was trying to learn to play golf, one of the Germans just shaking his head in amazement as I kept missing the ball and making huge divots on the course. Finally, he began following me and filling in the holes. I gave up golf after a few trials. I was fonder of active sports like swimming, tennis, badminton, and biking.

"Some of the nurses I knew were really dedicated, but many others seemed more concerned with their own lives than with those of their patients. The WAC medical technicians, who'd had been trained to draw blood, inject medications, dispense prescription drugs, and other things, did much of their work anyway. It seemed to me that many nurses just had a ball.

"When the Phillipines were liberated, and later after Japan surrendered, many of the men who survived the 'Bataan Death March,' including General Wainwright, were sent to us. They were so subdued, walking around as though in a fog, looking at their new surroundings as if they didn't understand that they were free and back in the States. It's difficult to say what they felt. They didn't talk about their experiences and we knew enough not to intrude on them. They all should have been given the Medal of Honor and pensioned-off for life."

Slow to begin to employ WACs, the Medical Department had, by the end of the war, become their largest employer, utilizing some 20,000 WACs, one-fifth of the entire Corps. It was not until early 1945 that General George Marshall directed that WAC Hospital Companies be organized. By the time these were staffed, the need for medical technicians was declining, and the WAC hospital companies were disbanded after V-J Day.

Civilian Workers and the Red Cross

Although the Ashford General Hospital was a military post — operated by Army personnel, for Army personnel, according to Army regulations — as many as five hundred civilians helped in its management. Most of these men and women qualified for and filled civil service positions. There were, in addition, scores of civilian Red Cross personnel, many of them full-time staff, others part-time volunteers.

Throughout the war, both at home and abroad, the Army hired civilians in order to free men and officers from essentially non-military assignments. At first, the substitution ratio was three civilians hired for each two soldiers replaced — reflecting the civilian eight-hour day versus the military's twelve-hour day. Later, a one-for-one substitution rule was adopted. Civilians with all levels of skills were employed, from junior clerks to medical and surgical consultants.

The Red Cross assigned many of its paid staff to hospitals, where they performed some invaluable services. They helped men with personal problems that might slow the diagnosis and treatment of wounds, provided comfort items and services, and directed various social activities. In countless other ways, the Red Cross was "always there" for the boys.

Full-time, paid Red Cross staff lived in the "Presidential Cottage," built in 1816 and dedicated over one hundred years later to the first eight Presidents who had visited the "Old White" over the years: Van Buren, Tyler, Taylor, Fillmore, Pierce, Buchanan, Grant, and Arthur. The Red Cross social service program was directed by Audrey Deniston, while the recreation program was directed by Irene Spitz. Each program director had a small full-time staff, and the support of various volunteers, such as the Gray Ladies. Wearing the gray uniforms that gave them their name, the Gray Ladies were members of local Red Cross chapters and devoted endless hours to the social service and recreational programs.

Martha Elizabeth Benjamin was one of the Gray Ladies. Her son, J.W. ("Ben") Benjamin, Jr. of Lewisburg, West Virginia, who was then attending the Greenbrier Military School, says:

"My mother was a very beautiful and popular Gray Lady at the hospital. Then in her late thirties, she was anxious to do what she could in the emergency. She completed what was then called the standard course in Red Cross Home Nursing and the prescribed training to be a member of the Red Cross Hospital and Recreation Corps.

"At Ashford, she wrote letters, ran endless errands, chatted and comforted, stitched insignia on uniforms, and patched up the occasional broken romance. It's easy to see why the boys loved her. Mother called her service at Ashford the happiest time of her life. At least two of her patients came back to see her in the 1980s, and others telephoned or wrote letters until her death in 1988."

Ashford Gray Lady, Martha Elizabeth Benjamin.

Sewing shoulder patches, enlisted men's stripes, hash marks, and other insignia on uniforms was a never-ending chore. The need for help with the stitching was such that a tiny alcove on the main floor of the hospital was converted into a "Gray Ladies' Sewing Service Center." Any member of the military could drop by for assistance, and a uniform that needed some repair could be left with the Gray Lady on duty. The service was begun by Mrs. Robert Clarke, wife of the Post Chaplain.

Ashford's first graduating class of Army-trained Red
Cross Nurse's Aides (courtesy Rosemary Dent).

Beulah "Boots" Lusk was living in Springdale, a small
town near Pittsburgh, Pennsylvania, when she went with a
girl friend to see the girl friend's brother, a patient at Ashford
General Hospital:

"Taking time off from my job at a beauty shop to visit
some distant military hospital didn't sound very exciting,
but I was twenty-four, and had never ridden a train, so finally I agreed to go. This was in February 1945. We took
the B&O to Washington, then changed to the 'Chessie' for
White Sulphur Springs. On the way I was primed to see a
military hospital like something in the movies — bare walls,
with antiseptic floors, and so on. Wow! When we walked
into that lobby, I felt like a complete country bumpkin: all of
those lovely chandeliers and mirrors, the G.I.s lounging
around in comfy chairs, even after-dinner organ music!

"We stayed a week at a motel in town, and out of curiosity I took a look at the hospital's beauty shop. One of the women told me they'd probably be needing another person soon but I said I already had a job in Pittsburgh.

"Meanwhile, during the week, I had met and become friendly with the roommate of my girl friend's brother. His name was Charles Carpenter. Four months later, I returned to Ashford to visit him. Charles had been thinking ahead, and told me right away that they had a job for me in the beauty shop. I went to work the very next morning.

"Charles had been a paratrooper with the 101st Airborne Division, dropping behind the German lines on D-Day. He was hit soon afterwards, and when I first met him, he had a hole through his arm and four inches of bone missing. But he was up and around, and getting stronger every day.

"At the shop, we worked on a commission basis, and I made good money. We got seventy-five percent of what the charge was. I did permanents and everything. 'Perms' ran ten to twenty dollars each. They put limits on what military personnel had to pay, but there were no limits for civilians. Some of the well-to-do people from town came in, and we'd charge them whatever we wanted to. Of course, most of my patrons were nurses and WACs. We opened at 8:00 A.M. and stayed open until we ran out of customers.

"The two other girls in the shop were the nicest young women you'd ever want to meet. Violet Jackson had been there the longest. She was from Fairfax, Virginia, and her husband was employed in the motor pool. Jane Cook came from Washington, Pennsylvania, and her husband was overseas. Our shop was on the lower lobby level, along with the commissary and the PX.

"My most famous customer didn't tell me who she was until I asked. When a WAC missed her appointment one morning, I was given this short, dumpy lady in a wide-brimmed felt hat and a floral-patterned white dress. I gave her a pleasant 'good morning,' but I thought 'who is this!' Her slip was showing and she was just a mess. She said she only wanted her hair done but would return the next morning for 'the works.' The whole time I worked on her, she talked about being overseas but didn't give her name. Finally, after I asked, she said 'I am Mrs. Wainwright.'

Gen. Jonathan Wainwright salutes Clyde Beck the day he was awarded his Brig. General's star (courtesy Bert O'Brien).

"Well, of course, she and her husband, General Wainwright, had only just returned from the Pacific theater where they had been prisoners of the Japanese. She explained that she hadn't had a chance to shop or to get herself fixed up. The next morning she came again, and as I did her fingernails I noticed how like a baby's nails they were. 'I apologize for my nails,' she said, 'but in prison all we got was rice and potatoes and my nails suffered.' General Wainwright brought her down to the shop that second morning, and that poor man really looked starved. No wonder they called him 'Skinny.'

"Charles Carpenter and I were married on June 15, 1946, just before the hospital closed. The chapel wasn't available, but Ashford Chaplain Mortimer Dean was sweet enough to marry us in the St. Thomas Episcopal Church in White Sulphur Springs. Looking back, I remember so much about Ashford, but the best part was making so many close friends. It was wonderful."

E. Warren Baker, who still works at The Greenbrier, was born in White Sulphur Springs. He was a student at Bolling High School in nearby Lewisburg (at the time, Greenbrier County's only high school for black youngsters) when he found a part-time job in Ashford's post exchange.

"The PX was open all day and always busy, but the busiest time of all was following the evening movie when so many of the soldiers crowded in. People sat at tables and chairs — there were no booths — and had sandwiches, hamburgers, and milkshakes, or potato chips and cokes and things like that. A White Sulphur Springs woman, Nelle Montague, operated the place with the help of five girls, another man, and me. We might get as many as a hundred and fifty customers in there at one time. My job was to clean off the tables, sweep the floor, and help around as needed.

"The German prisoners of war never used the PX. They weren't allowed to have U.S. money, and besides, they had a canteen of their own. I know they had a reputation for not liking blacks too well, but if there was any such problem there at the hospital, it must have been swept under the rug. I never saw evidence of it.

"The commissary, run by a man named Chuck Norvell, was just across the hall from the PX. There you could buy watches, toiletries, billfolds, small items of clothing, stationery, and lots of other things, and save yourself a walk to town. I remember the Chicken Shack that people talk about. A man named Slaughter ran it, and it was popular not just for its dance floor, but because it had slot machines.

"When the hospital closed, a lot of people hated to see the Army go. During the war, many had more or less got back on their feet thanks to the Army. Once the hospital was gone, wages immediately went back to the old hotel scales. After I graduated from high school, however, I went to work full-time at The Greenbrier and, except for my Army service from 1951 through 1953, I've been there happily ever since."

Ashford General Hospital had black patients as well as black employees. Although during World War II the army officially was segregated, numerous photographs of a variety of patient activities at Ashford indicate that soldiers recovering from wounds were disinclined to make distinctions on the basis of skin color. Despite how many individuals may have felt, the Army's policy was to offer occasional separate entertainment for the hospital's black patients. *The Ashford News* reported such events as dances held for "colored" patients and staff. An all-black band from Camp Lee, Virginia, provided the live music for one of these dances, then played for the all-white 3590th medical detachment dance the following night.

Frances Wright Wolf was born in Clifton Forge, Virginia, a town about forty miles east of White Sulphur Springs on the C&O mainline. After a year of business school in

Staunton, Virginia, she took a civil service test at Ashford and went to work there in February 1945.

"I was one of two secretaries in the neurosurgical office headed by Major George L. Maltby. The two of us constituted a 'typing pool' to handle most of the dictation given by the several doctors in the unit. We had old manual typewriters, of course, and had to make lots of carbons of everything. I did mostly correspondence and case histories — the opening and closing charts, and details about the medical treatment.

"Once the war in Europe was over, we got fewer neurosurgical cases and I was moved into the dermatological section headed by Lieutenant Colonel Herbert L. Traenkle. I didn't want to leave neurosurgery, but with more and more patients arriving with skin diseases the dermatology section had to have help.

"Like most of the single civil service girls, I lived in the Lester Building. It was great: I could walk to work in five minutes and had free maid service. Some bachelor officers' quarters were on the ground floor and I think the MPs had an office there as well. We civilians ate with the officers and went through the cafeteria line just as they did. We worked a forty-eight hour week, except when things were slow and we were let go on Saturday.

"I went to movies, dances, and parties and helped at the USO Club in White Sulphur Springs, and was even a cheerleader at basketball games. I was pretty good at Ping-Pong, too, and played everybody.

"I got to know a good many patients, and even dated some. There were POWs around on the floors, too, but I didn't get to know any very well. I did make friends with many nurses and WACs. It was a lot of fun, a part of my life I wouldn't take anything for."

The Lester Building was a three-story wood frame structure with a two-story attached annex built in 1808. Windows and doors opened to bannistered porches interconnected with stairways. The building stood a stone's throw away from the famous Springhouse. While the hospital's patients, staff, and visitors delighted in taking photos of the Springhouse, the Lester Building held no such allure.

The Lester Building, November 1950 (courtesy The Greenbrier).

Cathryn Mays Dodd grew up in Clifton Forge, and had just graduated from business school when she accepted work at Ashford as the post inspector's secretary:

"He seemed to go everywhere inspecting everything, including the POW camp. His main job, however, was with the Officer's Disability Retirement Board, which is where I did most of my work. They had lots of long meetings and I took minutes and dictation. I recall sharing my office with Lieutenant Walter Miller who was the hospital veterinarian. I went to some of the dances, and spent time in the game room, but I didn't get to know many patients. Some of us occasionally ate lunch or dinner downtown, mainly for the change of menu — the hospital served too much mutton. I enjoyed Ashford. I went back six years ago, and the place was just as beautiful as ever."

Maxine Flint Justice was born in Alderson, West Virginia, and says the Greenbrier was her "Sunday outing" as a child. She took a secretarial position in the hospital Registrar's Office in mid-1943:

"The Registrar's Office was near the swimming pool, on the lower level. When big groups of men arrived from the field hospitals, registration needed three of us, one man and two women, all of us working together. Arriving ambulatory patients lined up in the hallway to register with one of us and be assigned a room. We removed the EMT tags from their necks in order to copy certain information into our records. I have to laugh, remembering how gingerly we handled those tags — as though they might have had V.D. germs or something on them.

"Some of the boys were so happy to be home again, they couldn't say it enough times. After the invasion of Europe, our registration lines got longer and we became extra busy. The litter cases, of course, bypassed us, and went straight to the wards.

"After a year in the Registrar's Office, I was transferred to the Quartermaster Warehouse Office located in the horse stables area, just off U.S. 60 toward the airport. Several of the stables had been converted to QM warehouses while a little four-room caretaker's house had become headquarters. Among other things, we distributed the canned and dry food for the medical detachment (anything perishable was stored in the hospital's huge ice room). I typed requisitions and distribution records, making lots of carbon copies because we had no 'ditto' machine.

"A few of the German prisoners of war worked for us, and you could just see the hate in some of their eyes! The younger ones weren't so bad. They hadn't had as much

Maxine Flint with a warehouse worker and children (three barefoot) visiting from nearby White Sulphur Springs.

indoctrination as the older men. Once when a crew of them was painting our office, just to be aggravating, we all sang, 'There'll be a hot time in the town of Berlin, when the Yanks come marching in.' They got so angry!

"Though they weren't allowed to say anything to us, they

got even by lighting up the foul-smelling cigarettes they bought in their stockade canteen. By the end of the war, they were driving supply trucks and going off all over the place. There was so much going on that I seldom went home, even on weekends. I tried all the sports, and swung

Maxine Flint and QM Sgt. Erle Neubecker at the stables, with east-west U.S. Route 60 in the background.

my first tennis racquet there. Though we weren't supposed to date patients, we did. Working in the Registrar's Office, we had access to the patients' records, so if we met someone we liked, first we'd check him out to see if he was married and things like that.

"Whenever a group from the medical detachment was shipped out to an overseas assignment, we'd have a big party up at the NCO Club on Kate's Mountain. They'd wear full uniforms, with all their bags packed and waiting at the train station. We'd have a few drinks, then escort them back down the hill around midnight. Some guy would blow taps on a bugle as the boys boarded their train. It was sad because you didn't know if you'd ever see someone again."

The men and civil service employees of the Army Personnel Office. Master Sgt. Floyd M. Buesinger is far left; Capt. Lynn T. Rose is fifth from right in back row (courtesy of Shirley Fritchen, Capt. Rose's daughter).

The administrative officer in charge of Ashford's civilian personnel was Mrs. Mabel Tollett, a firm but fair executive, well-remembered and generally well-liked by Ashford's many "civil service girls." Although *The Ashford News* provided information about many individual civilians, Mrs. Tollett's employment office, and her dedicated supervision of 300 to 500 civilian employees, remained largely unheralded. That nearly half of Ashford's civilians were employed there for two years or more suggests how well they were selected and supervised.

The functions of the Army Personnel Office were considerably more complex. Captain Lynn T. Rose headed the office, assisted by 1st Lts. Roy Sibold and George R. Fortney, and twenty-two enlisted men. By mid-1944, while some enlisted men had been replaced by civilians, the entire staff had grown to thirty. The office consisted of seven departments: payroll, service records, classification, correspondence, discharges, reports and returns, and transportation. Work hours were 8:00 A.M. to 5:00 P.M. Monday through Saturday, and 8:00 A.M. to noon on Sundays.

Later in 1944, Lt. Sibold was promoted to captain and placed in charge of a new Personal Affairs Office that would handle such things as claims for benefits, insurance, legal aide, mustering-out pay, allotments, and similar subjects of great concern to patients and post personnel anticipating an early discharge. A sixteen-member women's volunteer committee was formed to serve as receptionists, and to provide information on maternity and child care, housing, women's activities and related problems.

Betty Watts Bergdoll grew up in Rupert, West Virginia, a small town on U.S. 60, west of White Sulphur Springs. After graduating from high school and passing the requisite civil service test she was employed in the Quartermaster's office at the horse stables. The first young woman to work there, she was known as "The Queen of the Stables."

"I was a clerk-typist doing correspondence, getting voucher orders out, filing, keeping books, sometimes hunting for wee errors of a few cents where the ledgers might be off. How I could have used a modern computer in those days! We might search for hours for pennies.

Betty Watts, when she was known as "The Queen of the Stables."

"I soon earned the respect of the men I worked with, so that after a curse word or dirty joke, there would be a sudden silence until someone stepped forward to apologize. Captain Howard D. Johnson was in charge, and all the men were great to work with.

"Jack Gillespie was Captain Johnson's right hand man and assistant. His desk was directly in front of the captain's and all the paperwork went through him. Before taking the job at Ashford, Jack had been a union official, and he was all business. He did a great job for us. He got along with everyone, and had a great sense of humor. Jack also was a fine gentleman and good family man. I think he was related to Ken Gillespie, the Mayor of White Sulphur Springs.

"The German prisoner of war camp was just down the road from us, and each morning they'd pass by in their trucks on their way to work around the hospital, and we'd hear them singing. For me, it was very uplifting. They arrived at the camp just after the Italian POWs moved out. Before they moved in, they cleaned, sprayed, and aired all the bedding in the sun. They scrubbed everything. The first time they had fresh corn they refused to eat it, calling it 'pig's food.' I never ordered it again.

Jack Gillespie, one of the key civilian employees at the Quartermaster Corps warehouses (courtesy Betty Watts Bergdoll).

"One of the prisoners was assigned to our office. Hans Ungerer was a brilliant fellow who learned English quickly. He would borrow my *Reader's Digest*, then question me about the words he didn't know. He kept our office spotless. He even asked for some flower seeds, and made a flower garden around our building. Hans believed that Germany would win the war until the day he saw photos of bombed-out Mannheim, his hometown, and knew all was lost. I had married and left Ashford before he was repatriated, but we kept in touch and long years later his family and mine exchanged visits, both here and in Germany. I'm sad to say that he's dead now.

Former POW, Hans Ungerer (courtesy Betty Watts Bergdoll).

"One day at work, I got a call from a soldier asking me for a date. I had only met him once and had seen that he was as bashful, or even more bashful, than I was. I realized from listening to the voice on the phone that it was another man calling for him. Johnny didn't have nerve enough to call me himself. I couldn't help feeling sorry for him, and we did date. He had been slightly crippled in a childhood accident and I was the first girl he'd ever dated. He kept bringing me gifts until I told him it wasn't necessary.

"One of my best friends at Ashford was Christine Jones, who worked in the Chaplain's Office. One of the things I liked was to attend Chaplain Robert Clarke's evening Bible studies held in the nice little hospital chapel. Colonel Clarke was an older man and made the Bible really come to life. He was a perfect Chaplain, so full of joy! He kept Christine busy when she had any spare time, typing out new jokes for a book he was compiling. I don't know if he finished it.

"I usually went home to Rupert on the weekends, often with my friend Clara Thompson, and we'd return to White Sulphur Springs late on Sunday. Returning to the Lester Building, we'd take a shortcut through a long, dark tunnel under the hospital. We were always scared we'd see a rat down there, because the tunnel was where the garbage was taken out. It was a completely localized problem and all the rest of the hospital was always absolutely spotless.

"One night, another friend and I invited our soldier-dates to come in the hall on the first floor. I guess our talking and laughing annoyed some people, and the next day, we were

The Greenbrier Stables were converted into QM warehouses, and the horses relocated to private farms. Sgt. Harlan "Shorty" Ganote, far right, was in charge (courtesy Betty Watts Bergdoll) .

called on the carpet. However, the happy outcome was that several rooms were made into a lounge where we could invite our dates in for coffee and cookies. Looking back, we fared wonderfully well, and the hospital has a very special place in my memory."

Betty Watts (r.) with her good friend Christine Jones (courtesy Betty Watts Bergdoll).

Christine Jones Madarasz, from nearby Ronceverte, graduated from business college in Bluefield. At Ashford, she was a secretary in the Chaplain's Office:

"I worked with three or four chaplains. There were usually two assigned to be available for Protestant patients and one for the Catholic patients. Jewish services were conducted by a rabbi from Charleston. One chaplain spoke good German and was active with the prisoners of war.

"My duties included keeping an up-to-date card file on each patient, with information on his religious preference, next of kin, age, marital status, room location in the hospital, and so forth. I prepared stencils and printed up the chapel bulletins, handled the correspondence and calls, ordered the supplies, and did all the other things a secretary does. All the chaplains' personal matters and minutes of meetings with patients were, of course, strictly confidential."

The Post Chapel was established in what had been the hotel's North Parlor. Each denomination held services there: Jewish services at 6:30 P.M., Fridays; Catholic masses at 7:00 A.M. weekdays, and at 6:15 A.M. and 9:00 A.M. Sundays; Protestant Sunday services at 10:30 A.M. "Chaplain's Chat,"a column in *The Ashford News*, provided information and inspirational messages. Free bibles were available to anyone at the hospital.

Clara Thompson Henderson, a graduate of Rupert High School, was nineteen when she went to work in the civilian personnel and payroll section. Her uncle, C.W. Thompson, had been the C&O ticket agent at The Greenbrier before the war and remained when it became a hospital. It was during a visit with her uncle that she accepted her job there:

"I worked in the civilian personnel and payroll office in what had been a barroom near the ballroom. The horseshoe-shaped bar still remained, with our desks and chairs behind it. One of our big jobs was processing the civilian payroll every other Friday. We often worked late to get it to Fifth Service Command Headquarters in Columbus, Ohio, on time. We typed the whole thing, hundreds and hundreds of names, with everyone's gross earnings and deductions. When the checks came back, they were disbursed by the officers in charge of each hospital section.

"Everyone had to take out something in war savings bonds. Not necessarily a whole bond, but some amount towards one. I typed all that information too. Some employees said they could barely make ends meet after deductions. There wasn't any bank at Ashford. People had to go downtown to deposit or cash their checks.

Clara Henderson worked for over two years in the civilian personnel office.

"I met and got to know Sam Snead, and I took lessons at the swimming pool, and saw Esther Williams do her aquacade show there. I also saw Les Brown and his 'Band of Renown' play in the hospital theater. These stars all had their meals in the main dining room, and we often had tables next to them.

"I went to two or three dances at the Casino, attended some of the USO shows, and during their visit I saw the Duke and Duchess of Windsor. I also wrote my high school sweetheart lots of letters. While he was on leave after returning from Europe, he came to White Sulphur Springs and we got married in the hospital chapel. When the war ended, and my husband left service, I resigned. I'd been at Ashford twenty-seven months."

The purchase of war bonds was encouraged by editorial items in *The Ashford News*. One such, from January 18, 1944, even suggested this New Year's resolution: "I RE- SOLVE TO INVEST EVERY DOLLAR I CAN SPARE IN WAR BONDS." War bonds could be purchased at the hos- pital post office or at army pay tables. Recovering patients on leave from the hospital campaigned in Virginia and West Virginia and helped to raise $1,000,000 in bond sales.

In a December 1945 ceremony in the hospital's theater, Gen. Beck congratulated Ashford's civilian employees for winning the War Department's coveted "Bond Flag." This meant that ninety-five percent of them had purchased bonds in the most recent drive. Even better results had been pro- duced while the war was still going on: every civilian em- ployee had bought a bond, thereby winning the Treasury Department's "E Flag."

Mary A. Hanna was twenty-nine, and a resident of Covington, Virginia when she accepted a clerical job in an office that was shared by Quartermaster and Signal Corps personnel. She worked there from January 1943 until the hospital closed.

"My boss was Signal Corps First Lieutenant Joseph J. Rein, Jr. I took care of phone bills, wrote orders for added phone service, accounted for the phones and phone jacks in all the rooms, and typed great amounts of correspon- dence. It was an 8-to-5 job, five days a week, and most weekends I went home. I didn't have a car, but I could always ride with a friend. There were two women in the Signal Corps Office and perhaps a half dozen in the Quartermaster's Office. It was all just one big office, really, and we'd help each other when things backed up — which could be pretty often.

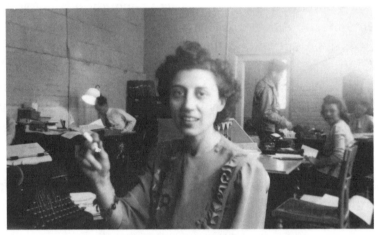

Mary Hanna worked in the Quartermaster Office,

"I went to some of the dances and the movies, and saw a few of the visiting dignitaries. We weren't allowed on the upper floors where the patients were, but it was nice meeting them when they were downstairs or out on the grounds. Time passed so quickly I can't remember half of what I did there. I know I hated to leave the place. I loved it."

Mary Ellen Sparks Given was born and raised in Richwood, West Virginia, youngest of three children. After passing the civil service test for secretary, she was invited to Ashford for an interview. While her parents at first said, "No way will our little girl go down there with all those soldiers," her pleas finally won them over. They drove her there, sat in on her interview, and agreed she could take the job:

"My first boss was Major Robert P. Kelly, hospital Chief of Orthopedics. He was a real southern gentleman from Atlanta, had a big drawl, and was a pleasure to be around. I worked hard but played hard, too. I especially liked to play Ping-Pong with the patients. I tried tennis once — my first and last lesson ever. We did lots of bicycling after work, and I enjoyed bowling in the downtown lanes.

Mary Ellen Sparks was secretary to Maj. Robert Kelly, Chief of Orthopedics; Col. Beck's Casino Cottage is in the right background.

"I met so many people from all over the country, and that was fun and educational, too. The German prisoners of war were very interesting to me. They ran some of the elevators and I'd talk with them in the elevator going up to my sixth floor office. One young man, only sixteen years old, made a bracelet for me, engraved with my nickname, 'Sparkie.' I've kept it all these years. Thinking about Ashford has brought back such a flood of good memories!"

Mildred Ellis grew up in Ronceverte, West Virginia, attended the two-year Greenbrier College for Women, and earned a B.S. degree at St. Joseph's College in Emmitsburg, Maryland. She went to Mercy Hospital in Baltimore for additional training, but, at her father's request, instead of taking a job there, she came home. She took a position in the Ashford laboratory and remained there from September 1943 until May 1946:

"When I first came to work in the Ashford laboratory, with about twenty of the men from the Medical Detachment, I was the only woman there. Later, many of the men were replaced by WACs. Although my job was civil service, I

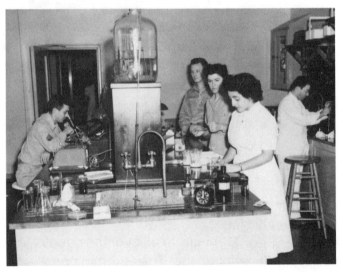

Hematology Department, lab technicians Abe Prostic, Steve Conway, Reuben Bradlyn, and Mildred Ellis (right foreground), with 2nd Lt. Jane Krisberg, 1944 (courtesy Mildred Ellis).

didn't have to take a test because of my college background. Our boss was Major William A. Antopol, chief of the lab service. His successor, just before the hospital closed, was another doctor, Lieutenant Colonel Oscar J. Wollenman. I went around the hotel daily to draw blood samples from patients the doctors had earmarked for testing. I wore a white uniform and lab coat, and carried a little tray with syringes and other necessary paraphenalia. An enlisted man came along to help. The patients with malaria were a real challenge. When they were having an attack, they trembled so violently their whole bed would shake. Getting a blood sample was sometimes very difficult.

Maj. William A. Anapol and M/Sgt. Chivers Woodruff in the Major's office, 1944 (courtesy Mildred Ellis).

"The boys coming back from the South Pacific, especially those who had been prisoners of the Japanese, had all sorts of problems. I talked with a man who'd survived the Bataan death march, and he looked like a walking stick. I remember one emotionally disturbed patient always searching the tree tops with his eyes, looking for enemy snipers. I don't know if the records show it, but one patient hanged himself from a window. As great in many ways as Ashford was, it had its share of tragedies just as all military hospitals did.

The Chemistry Department, Bill "Red" Mattox, Eugene Hoffman, and Charlie Miller at work (courtesy Mildred Ellis).

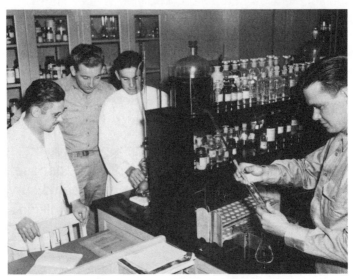

The Urinalysis Department, Justin Meyers, Bob Adams, and Ralph Wilkes, 1st Lt. Robert W. Johnson looking on (courtesy Mildred Ellis).

"But so many lives were saved, too. When I was in the hematology section, I had a patient whose illness seemed to defy diagnosis. The doctors knew he had malaria, but he'd blackout for no known reason. In studying one of his blood samples, I discovered that the patient had a very rare form of malaria, and that the malarial parasites were literally clogging the arteries in his brain. When I reported what I'd found, the doctors were grateful indeed.

"We had a sick bay for the seriously ill German POWs. Many said they had never wanted to be in the war, but we had one tough little Nazi, all of fourteen years old, who'd tell us how Germany was winning. We had to threaten to return him to the Russian front to shut him up.

"The lab had windows opening onto the gardens on the north side of the hospital, and I'd see the POW work details pass by every day. I'd often hear them singing 'Heidi Marie' as they marched. They got the idea that I liked it, and they'd sing especially loud as they went past the lab windows.

"I really enjoyed the wartime ballads, such as 'I'll Be Seeing You,' 'Don't Sit Under the Apple Tree,' and 'I'll Walk Alone.' Even now when I hear them, they always bring back pleasant memories of those years when we were all a little more innocent.

"I've always loved animals, and at Ashford we had all kinds. The lady who ran the PX across from the lab brought her dog with her every day. A patient found a terrapin on the golf course one day and presented it to me as a gift. I kept it in my room in one of the Alabama Row cottages, and was quite careful where I put my toes in the morning when I got out of bed. One day it was missing. The maid had chased it outside. Another time, I found some frog eggs down near the lake, and brought them home to see them hatch. When the maid disposed of them, too, I was terribly angry with her.

"There was always so much to do. There were dances for the patients, and we'd teach some of them the steps. Many of the boys also liked to go into the town and often did so without the required pass. They'd just step over the low-cut hedge to avoid the sentry box at the main gate. I'd see them all over town with their crutches and canes, many with casts and walking irons.

WACs Edna Hickman, Florence Ballin, Gladys Liles, and Mary Barrett, and Mildred Ellis (r.) before picnic, September 1945.

"For me, my nearly three years at Ashford General Hospital were an unforgettable experience — a moving and terribly important one."

Dennis Dean, born in 1904 near Neola, West Virginia, lived through the great influenza epidemic of 1918, and had worked for twenty years in the lumber industry before accepting his job with the hospital fire department:

"As I recall, we had about twenty men altogether. Nine men would stand duty for twenty-four hours, then have the next day off, while another nine fellows were on duty. The two other men worked more or less regularly at the prisoner of war camp. Our boss was Chief Lloyd M. Steele, who had been the fire chief over in Covington. He was a demanding guy, but always fair.

Army-built fire station, Presidential Cottage atop hill in the background (courtesy Mary Ellen Sparks Given).

"One of my jobs each shift was to walk through the hotel — through every floor and every wing — and check the closets, supply rooms, and trash cans for possible fire hazards. Even though the hotel had a good sprinkler system, any fire might have been disastrous. I started on the top floor and worked down. If I found anything hazardous, I immediately reported it to the chief. We never had a fire that I know of, though once we were called out on a Sunday morning to fight a blaze at the Methodist Church in town. We fought it 'til noon, but it was bad, and pretty much destroyed the church.

"Whoever was on duty at midnight also would have to get a car and drive down around the Casino and then go in and all through it. Then drive up Kate's Mountain and check out the NCO Club. I didn't care much for those jobs.

"Once a week, we'd go out on a practice run. Take a truck down to the Casino, hook it up and throw water for half an hour or so. Later, we had to take off the hoses, uncouple and dry and then clean them. When we had a practice fire, I rode the back step of the truck, and I'd jump

Fireman Dennis Dean and his 1936 Plymouth.

off before the truck stopped — holding the end of the hose — then give it a couple of quick wraps round the fireplug to keep the truck from pulling it away. The idea was to see how quick we could do that and then get the water turned on.

"We had three trucks, two big ones, and a smaller one used mainly to fight brush fires. I was assigned to the smaller one. Every time we took a truck out of the garage, whether it was for practice or not, we had to wash the whole thing when we got back. We also had to check batteries and oil and run up the engines daily. On Sundays we skipped all that because the chief stayed home all day.

"I was there a total of thirty-one months, from late 1943 until April or May of 1946. I still remember that the badge number on my uniform cap was '14.' We didn't talk with the soldiers that much. We sort of stayed to ourselves. In fact, they didn't want us talking to them too much — they said it distracted us from our duties. When Ashford closed, I worked for another twenty-five years as the local game warden."

During the busiest months of 1945, the hospital oper-ated forty-five vehicles: various cars and trucks, including the fire engines, and three olive-drab, fourteen-passenger Army buses. The "buses" were actually a kind of long-wheel-base limosine used to shuttle patients about the grounds, and to and from downtown White Sulphur Springs. Avail-able only to the hospital's military personnel, they left from the north hospital entrance on the hour and returned on the half-hour with stops at the Casino and the hospital's main entrance.

Robell B. Clark, from Beckley, West Virginia, joined the Army in 1941 and served two years before receiving a medical discharge. He worked in a textile mill, then took a position in the supply department at Ashford General on July 5, 1945. He remained there for more than a year:

"We handled everything from drugs and surgical and dental equipment and supplies right down to household furniture. Due to the size of the hospital, supplies were trucked in almost every day and about every ten days we'd get one or two boxcar loads from the local freight office. To store and dispense everything, we had besides myself, two other civilians, a soldier, and three German POWs.

"One of our warehouse rooms was under the hospital's North Wing, in the basement. It was about fifteen-feet square and had concrete walls and a metal door that was kept

Medical detachment men and civilian employees at the Kate's Mountain NCO Club (courtesy Shirley Fritchen).

padlocked. We kept all alcohol, ether, and similar materials there. On one occasion when we went inside, there was a really strong odor of ether. The ether came twelve or eighteen cans to a case, and since none of the cans appeared damaged, we tried weighing them all to find which was leaking. That failed and I was told to empty all of the cans down an outdoor storm drain. Well, it was mid-summer, and the patients had their windows open. By the time I got to the fifth can every one of them had been slammed shut.

"One of my other jobs was to meet the hospital trains

that came in with loads of patients, and to give the staff clean linens — sheets, pillow cases, towels, and wash cloths — in exchange for the soiled ones. Also, I had to make sure the surgical department had plenty of oxygen. Still another job was mailing pay checks to patients home on leave.

"When there was furniture to be picked up or delivered in town or in Lewisburg, the three POWs and I did it. They were just like the boys next door. One was highly trained in radio and adapted a government issue radio so it picked up broadcasts from Germany. They listened to speakers say how *der Vaterland* was still winning the war, but, really, they knew better.

"The supply department was among the last group of people to leave Ashford because we were the ones who were shipping out everything the Army wanted to keep. I think I was almost the final person. By then I'd made arrangements to transfer into a U.S. Corps of Engineers unit assigned to the Bluestone Dam in Hinton, West Virginia. I look back on Ashford as a good place to have worked."

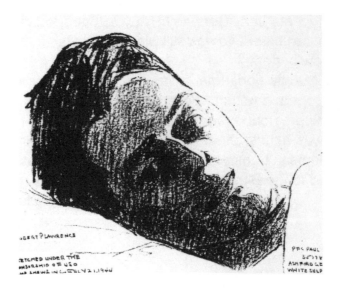

7

TOWNSPEOPLE AND VISITORS

During its almost four years of existence, Ashford attracted an estimated 50,000 visitors. In addition to the friends and families of patients, thousands of others came to entertain, instruct, and comfort. In 1945 alone, there were people from six hundred organizations — the American Legion and similar veterans' groups, various men's and women's business groups, service clubs, professional societies, and church and school groups. Many made repeated visits, staging concerts, shows, and entertainments throughout the year. A third category of visitors included celebrities and professional entertainers traveling with USO shows and all-army theatrical groups.

Marge Gillespie Carte of White Sulphur Springs was a unique visitor who fit into none of those categories:

"I was in seventh grade when I began to develop a problem in my left hip joint. My father, Kenneth Gillespie, was mayor of White Sulphur Springs and our home was across the street from the Hines Apartment Building. Dr. James Riley was one of the Ashford doctors living there, and every day he'd see me on my way to school, walking with great difficulty. One night, with my parents' permission, he smuggled me into the Ashford X-ray unit and took pictures of the joint. Instead of rheumatic fever, as a general practitioner had diagnosed, he discovered something much worse. Dr. Riley said that I should get to a specialist quickly.

Kenneth Gillespie, Mayor of White Sulphur Springs, was the owner of a small apartment house in which several "Ashford families" lived (courtesy Erich Steiner).

"Since there were no orthopedic surgeons within 150 miles at that time, my parents took me clear to Richmond for surgery. I returned to my 'hospital room' at home, and there I stayed encased in a body cast for three months, while the corrected joint healed and permanently set. Afterwards there was yet another 'smuggling caper.' I think Dr. Riley also arranged that the Ashford technicians would remove my cast, and take more X-rays for the Richmond surgeon. No one ever admitted it, but he likely managed the whole thing.

"My parents and I have always thought that had it not been for Dr. Riley and his correct diagnosis, I'd have been badly crippled throughout my teens, and after I'd turned eighteen, the damage would have been beyond repair.

"My older sister worked in the steno pool at the hospital, and through her, a lot of fellows in the orthopedic section learned about my operation and convalescence. I had a phone beside my bed at home and it wasn't unusual for some of the guys who were confined to bed to just call and talk. A few of those who were strung up in traction were encouraging to me, telling me how good it would be when I could get up and walk again. As a kid of thirteen, it was important for me to believe that, and maybe it helped them to think positively, too.

"Some of the fellows sent me things they'd made as part of their therapy, funny little gifts like model airplanes and braided leather bracelets. A therapist from the hospital came around and taught me to tint photographs. Though the patients and the staff were up there in the hospital, they were part of our community too and that was kind of nifty."

Many of Ashford's patients, especially those bedridden for extended periods of time, enjoyed making things with their hands: airplane and ship models, pen and ink or water color drawings, and clay models. Others became collectors, and at least one G.I. turned his hobby into a business. Cpl. Rosco O. Jackson of Coffeeville, Kansas,

wounded by machine gun fire on New Guinea and bedridden for more than a year, began collecting fountain pens.
Soon, he had collected three thousand of them, and started
to repair broken pens for his friends. Before he knew it, he
had established a pen repair service. On a good day, reported *The Ashford News*, Cpl. Rosco might take in twenty-
five dollars. The Chesapeake & Potomac Telephone Company of West Virginia was among his regular customers.

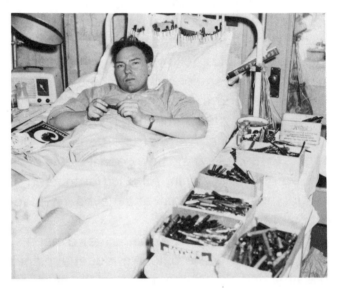

The Ashford News called him the "Nation's Favorite Pen-Up
Boy." Cpl. Rosco O. Jackson enjoyed collecting and fixing fountain pens (courtesy J.W. Benjamin, Jr.).

Most White Sulphur Springs residents did all they could
to make Ashford patients and staff feel at home: holding
dances for them in the high school gymnasium, giving them
doughnuts and coffee in the USO, inviting them for home-
style dinners, and treating them hospitably in downtown
shops, restaurants, and bars. Some hospitality may have

been overdone. A front-page *White Sulphur Springs Sentinel* story, "Let's Co-Operate With Ashford," described the good things done, but sounded a note of caution:

> Word has come to us, officially, that patients quite often go back to the hospital from down town in an intoxicated condition, possibly from having [been treated to] "one beer too many." This makes it difficult for the doctors there to keep an accurate check on their physical status, which also makes it unfair to both patients and medical staff.

Virginia Morgan Kahoe, like her niece Marge Gillespie, lived in White Sulphur Springs. She had worked at The Greenbrier while still in high school, went to Dunsmore Business School in Roanoke, but in late 1941, was again at work in the hotel accounting office. When the Japanese and German diplomats were interned there, she became the manager of the Gillespie Flower Shop. The owner, Mayor Kenneth Gillespie, refused to enter the building while the Germans were in residence:

"I remember very well when the diplomats came. I was born in 1906, so I was already in my thirties and not intimidated by any of them. Some of them would come down to the lower level to buy flowers, and I remember conversations with the German ambassador and with some high-ranking Japanese, too. So soon after Pearl Harbor, I had some difficulty being civil to the Japanese. Some of my diary entries from those days remind me what an unusual time it was:

> Christmas, 1941: This is a strange holiday season . . . we are at war. Here in our midst are 300 German people, being held until they can safely be returned to Germany. Perhaps some of them are sad today. At least I know I feel sad for them. They are polite and nice to work with. Have had a big season in the flower shop. . . . Some of the

newcomers I've met and talked with were brought in from Central America, among them a few young men with fencing scars on their cheeks. . . .

Feb. 21, 1942: After two months of being shut up all day with the German, Italian, Hungarian and Bulgarian people, I am beginning to talk and act like a foreigner. . . . Asked the F.B.I. and the U.S. Border Patrol guards to let me bring Mr. _____ home to lunch, but they refused. . . . The Naval Attache from Italy has decorated his room for a cocktail party. . . . More people arrived from Ellis Island and from Mexico, including 33 women and children. They were supposed to be gone by now, but it may be a long long time, as our Ambassadors are still in Germany, etc. . . .

May 18, 1942: The Japs are still here, though most of the Germans left on May 4th for New York to sail for Lisbon. Mr. _____ gave me his picture and a vanity case for farewell. Mr. _____ gave me a lovely manicure set. One of the most perfect gentlemen I ever met. Someday when this is all over he says he will come back and take me to dinner, or perhaps I will go to Munich? Mr. _____ came to say goodbye and brought a box of candy from Mrs. _____ .

"Later on, when the Army bought the hotel, I volunteered to help however I could. I was put to work taking an inventory of everything in the hotel, right down to the last bedsheet. I guess they had to have a record of what they'd paid three million and some dollars for. Once the hospital really got going, I worked in the medical supplies department. Another girl and I rented a small apartment in town, and an officer who lived near us gave us rides back and forth every day.

"What was really fun, though, was taking over the management of the White Sulphur Springs USO. (Mildred Tomlinson was the first director.) The building was just a tiny place, a one-story frame building with a covered porch and a sign saying 'USO' in foot-high letters. There were trees all around it, and in summer you could sit out on the grass in canvas lawn chairs. There was a small bar where the soldiers could buy cokes for ten cents each, and talk to the counter girls. It was comfortable and intimate.

Virginia Kahoe managed the local USO Club in 1946

"We kept it open every night, plus weekends, and I usually went over early so I could fix sandwiches and refreshments. Nearly every girl in town came over to talk and dance with the boys. Whenever there was a special party, for instance, on Valentine's Day, people in town would send us pies and cakes. Somebody's birthday was generally cause for a big party too.

"Most of the boys were patients from the hospital, though of course, we had a few soldiers and sailors from White Sulphur Springs who were just home on leave. At Christmas, we had a great big tree and little gifts for everyone. Most of the fellows who came were nearly well, but many came on crutches or in wheelchairs just to listen to the music, and watch the others dance to the juke box.

Inside the White Sulphur Springs USO Club (courtesy Virginia Kahoe).

"We had a piano and there was a little room in the back where we could seat twenty people at a time. We never had a bit of trouble with anyone. The boys from the hospital were beautifully behaved. And they were so appreciative. There were some serious romances, and I think at least three of our girls married patients. I managed the USO for about a year, and enjoyed every minute of it."

William E. Stark was one of the West Virginia State Troopers assigned to protecting the enemy diplomats interned at The Greenbrier in early 1942.

Neither Virginia Morgan Kahoe nor anyone else in the village of White Sulphur Springs thought that the interned diplomats posed any threat. After all, they were well guarded. William E. Stark was one of the more than thirty West Virginia State Police troopers assigned to Ashford:

"Though my memory of events there are rather hazy, I recall some of our specific instructions: we were not to engage in conversation about the war, unless the diplomats themselves brought up the subject. Our primary goal was to protect the diplomats from harassment by local or area residents, not to prevent them from escaping. Following the Japanese assault at Pearl Harbor, there was a considerable war hysteria, and 'incidents' involving the diplomats were to be avoided.

"Another of our instructions was to be extremely correct and to display courtly politeness. We all remained conscious of how we hoped that American diplomats in enemy hands would be treated.

"The diplomats were well informed about the United States and especially liked to talk about sports. I remember one man asking about a medal I was wearing. He'd noticed that none of the other troopers had one. When I told him that I was a member of the West Virginia State Police Pistol Team and had won the Distinguished Pistol Medal at the national shooting matches held annually at Camp Perry, Ohio, he had to know all about it."

The ambulatory Ashford patients could walk to the USO in downtown White Sulphur Springs by themselves, but often were accompanied on longer trips by donors who provided cars, buses, and even airplanes. On one occasion in October 1943, forty-two patients, nurses, and officers were treated to a great night out in Charleston by the Galperin Music Company and the Elks Club. Traveling by bus, they arrived just in time to enjoy dinner and then attend a performance of an opera by Gounod at the Charleston Civic Auditorium. They returned to White Sulphur Springs the same night, probably happy but undoubtedly exhausted from the long round trip.

For most patients, football was far more entertaining than opera. A chartered bus took twenty-eight men to Lexington, Virginia, to watch the 1945 Thanksgiving game between the Virginia Polytechnic Institute (VPI) and Virginia Military

Institute. Another thirty patients went to Roanoke to see the University of Virginia play VPI. Still another group journeyed to Charleston to see a West Virginia University game. The gridiron highlight of the year — at least for those who got to go — was the Pittsburgh Steelers v. the Washington Redskins game on December 2, 1945. George P. Marshall, owner of the Washington team, donated thirty tickets, and round-trip transportation in two Army C-47s was arranged by Ashford's Special Services unit in cooperation with the Red Cross.

Sports were important not only to the hospital's patients, but to the post personnel as well. In addition to its well-known basketball team, Ashford had a notable softball team as well. Kyle Gwinn was a 15-year-old schoolboy living in Hinton when he saw the team play an exhibition game in Oak Hill. That day, the Ashford pitcher, Cpl. Harold Blumke, was untouchable:

"Blumke was a professional softball pitcher from the Detroit area, and at Oak Hill he challenged anybody to come down from the stands and see if they could get a hit off him. Well a couple of dozen fellows lined up, using bats supplied by the Ashford team. After Blumke struck out seven or eight of them, without giving up even a foul tip, the rest just returned to the stands. The Ashford team also came here to play the Hinton All-Stars once. My high school coach was on that team, but Ashford beat them easily."

Jack Carte was a teenager whose family ran the Hotel Hart in White Sulphur Springs. It was nearly always filled with the families and friends of men at the hospital:

"Walter Pidgeon stayed with us when he visited Ashford in February 1945. We didn't have plumbing in the rooms, so he used the public bath next to my room. He sang in the shower, and sounded just like he did in the movies. The first time I heard him, I ran downstairs to tell my mom and pop, and then we all went up to listen in the hallway. The editor of our high school newspaper, Alma Woodrum, inter-

Fourteen-year-old Jack Carte delivered newspapers at Ashford, and had the thrill of shaking General Eisenhower's hand.

viewed him. I don't know if she heard much of what he said, because as he stood next to her at the officer's registration counter, he held her hand the whole time. Of course, I was just as goggle-eyed as she was. Pidgeon was a swell guy, and he stayed with us three or four nights.

"I was something of a mascot around the hospital, because I delivered the morning newspaper, *The Charleston Gazette*. It was a good deal, and I helped put my sister through college with the proceeds. I carried maybe 200 papers on weekdays, making three or four bike trips with the wire basket on the handlebar chock full. On rainy days, pop helped me with his car, dropping me and my papers off at the main entrance.

"I'd put my papers on two chairs in the main lobby near the dining room. I could leave them there and walk away any time I wanted to, and the men would drop change and bills on top, according to the honor system. On Sundays, I sold about 500 copies. I had the run of the hospital and delivered papers upstairs to the bedridden men. I was even allowed into the psychiatric ward, with never a problem. The patients there were just mixed-up, harmless men.

"Each morning, I delivered Colonel Beck's paper personally. Once when General Eisenhower was visiting the hospital, some of the patients distracted me from my routine until they saw 'Ike' go into the colonel's office. When I went in, I gave Colonel Beck a copy, and then another to 'Ike.' The patients had paid for Eisenhower's copy, and had warned me to not let him pay.

"The patients also told me that when I met the general I was to be sure to shake his hand. They said, 'Now when you come out don't let anyone touch your right hand.' I came out with my hand up in the air just like they said. They'd ripped off one side of a cigar box so I could stick my hand inside. The lid was lettered, 'This hand shook General Eisenhower's. One look, one dollar!' That was the kind of humor the men had. They were like gods to me, and they were so brave.

"Many knew they'd never walk again, but not once did I ever see anyone cry, or even act sorry for himself. I was young for my age, you know, pretty naive. In their way, a lot of the men helped me grow up. They'd tell me about their wives and families and their girl friends. Foul language was never used in my presence. Lots of the men would give me a little tip with the price of the paper, often an extra nickel, and in January they'd give me a birthday gift.

"After school, I used to go up to the hospital to do things for them, like run errands or whatever. I'd push the men in wheelchairs down to the Casino or to the gym. Many were too badly hurt or just too weak to move themselves.

"A nice thing for me was that I got to use the swimming pool. Charles Norelius took me as a student, but because I wanted to swim underwater more than I wanted to do the fancy stuff, he turned me over to his daughter Martha.* The best swimmers at Ashford put on several aquatic shows. In a South Sea 'fantasy' I played King Neptune, and my sister Alice was an island princess. I later put my swim training to good use as a Navy frogman during the Korean War."

Jack Carte was so well known at the hospital that the editor of *The Ashford News* asked him to describe "in his own words" his thoughts about the war and the men he saw each day. He wrote in the February 25, 1944 issue:

> I didn't know there was a war on until I started to sell papers here . . . I thought that war was just a game, and a game that you could have fun in; but, I believe I have a different idea now that I have seen patients with arms and legs off, with shrapnel wounds, and, oh, you just can't begin to imagine how some of the boys are messed up. . . [But] I'll tell you, those boys are full of excitement; even though they have lost brothers and pals in the war, side by side they still have that old American spirit, and, brother, if you don't believe me, ask them so and I am sure that they will say they still have the old spirit.

* Martha Norelius won gold medals at both the 1924 and 1928 Paris Olympics in the 400-meter event. In her time, she was regarded as the strongest female swimmer in the world.

Beatrice Richardson Leist visited Ashford General Hospital as a 12-year-old seventh grader from nearby McDowell County, West Virginia. She drove to White Sulphur Springs with her mother, an accomplished musician who taught piano and voice privately, then taught music in the public schools for some twenty-five years. Her mother was to sing for the patients while young Bea accompanied her at the piano. It was their first public performance together.

Twelve-year-old Bea Richardson and her mother.

"I have no idea how arrangements were made for the visit, whether it was through one of the civic clubs in our town, or through some other avenue. I know mother was more than happy to go, and at twelve, I was overwhelmed by the whole experience. I felt awed seeing so many wounded men.

"I think our trip was during the week (father would've been along had it been a Saturday or Sunday) and it was so hot it must have been summertime. I don't know what I wore, except that I thought I looked nice, even though rumpled a bit from riding in the car. I was terribly excited, wondering what to expect and how things would go.

"The piano they rolled out for us was so small I was afraid it didn't have eighty-eight keys. Since mother was primarily a classical musician, her repertoire consisted mostly of art songs and some operatic favorites. But she also sang 'Smoke Gets In Your Eyes' and the men enjoyed it so much they asked for an encore.

"I've often returned to the Greenbrier over the years, and had no sense of *deja vu.* But once in a while, after entering the grounds and seeing the main building surrounded by all those trees, memories do return."

For recovering patients, learning to like good music was an activity encouraged by the staff of the reconditioning unit. Daily one-hour music appreciation classes offering the best of the classics, both instrumental and vocal, began in 1945. According to *The Ashford News,* those hours were "filled with the music that you want and know, the music that you would like to know more about, and the music that will become one of the richest experiences of your life." An Ashford Glee Club and a Chapel Choir were formed for those who were more interested in singing.

Besides listening to popular and classical music played on the organ or the record player in the organ room, patients could hear music on individual radios in their rooms. Many radios were donated: in mid-1943, Charleston citizens sent fifty at one time, and families and friends provided still others. A master aerial, with connections to serve all the radios in the hospital, was installed in 1944, in order to improve the reception of more distant stations. A central system that allowed patients to listen to any of four "piped-in" stations was introduced the next year.

Lt. Colonel Joseph W. Benjamin taught at the Greenbrier Military School in Lewisburg and was the school's public relations officer and its alumni secretary. His son, J.W. Benjamin, Jr., described those days:

"My father was the head of the school's English Department for many years, coached its tennis and golf teams, and was the director of publications. He still found time to

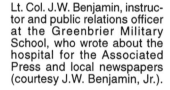

Lt. Col. J.W. Benjamin, instructor and public relations officer at the Greenbrier Military School, who wrote about the hospital for the Associated Press and local newspapers (courtesy J.W. Benjamin, Jr.).

visit Ashford General, writing literally hundreds of stories about wounded G.I.s and other hospital events. He was a 'stringer' for the Associated Press, and his stories appeared in newspapers all over the country.

"I believe he became involved with Ashford through Captain Robert Parker, an affable man who directed the hospital's Special Service unit. Dad became highly knowledgeable about Ashford and was able to meet Generals Eisenhower, Clark, and Wainwright there. He invited General Wainwright to come to Lewisburg and review us cadets. How excited we were! He came with General Beck and was met by our Colonel J.M. Moore, the Greenbrier Military School's superintendent. In his address after we passed in review for him, the 'Hero of Bataan' bore down heavily on integrity, and we were deeply impressed.

"As for me and some of the other cadets, we went over to Ashford several times. In particular, I recall the school's chess team, on which I played the first position, competing against a team of patients and winning. But on the return to Lewisburg, our taxi encountered a sudden snowstorm, and we were exactly one minute late checking back into school. For this infraction, we drew penalty tours and had to pace so many times around the courtyard at rigid attention. But no one complained. We had beaten the veterans!"

John A. Arbogast, a native of Greenbrier County, comes from a family prominent in western Virginia since before the Civil War.* A local businessman, he remembers the day the German prisoners of war came to town.

"Most town residents were skeptical by nature, but curious. So when the news broke that some captured German prisoners were arriving at the C&O train station, everyone turned out to get a good look. I think we were all surprised.

---

* His grandfather, John W. Arbogast, served four years with the Confederate 14th Virginia Cavalry, and fought in 1863 in the Battle of White Sulphur Springs. Hundreds of Confederate dead are buried throughout Greenbrier County, including some in a small graveyard on The Greenbrier's grounds.

Instead of the haughty and defiant faces we expected, we saw mostly young men wearing big smiles, obviously glad to be captives here. As they marched away to the prison camp, they struck up joyful songs about returning home safely from the war.

John Arbogast (l.) on the golf course with Father Felix Kirsch.

"Many months later, I was playing golf on one of the Greenbrier's courses with Father Felix Kirsch who taught language and religion in Washington, D.C. As we reached the first green, we met three young German POWs attending to the grass. When Father Felix spoke to them in German — he'd been born there — they were so happy. One of the lads wept tears of joy when he learned that Father Felix was from his own home town. It was a heartwarming moment. Those boys were so young and so homesick that you couldn't help feeling sorry for them even though they were the enemy."

Elizabeth Jones Greever was from Bluefield, West Virginia, and during the 1944-1945 school year was in her sophomore year at the Greenbrier College for Women:

"We Greenbrier College girls spent lots of time at Ashford. We went to monthly dances held for all of the men who'd had birthdays during the month. There would be punch, and soft drinks and sandwiches, and a cake. A live band provided the dance music. Each of us dressed up in her best evening gown and an Army bus came to the school to pick us up.

"The music was typical '40s — Tommy Dorsey, Benny Goodman, and Glenn Miller — and the band mixed the upbeat with the slower selections. The men in wheelchairs didn't dance, of course, but sat on the sidelines and watched. Some of the men with arm or leg casts danced, and did well, considering, not that it mattered, as long as they enjoyed themselves. A few girls would always stand and talk with those who didn't dance. We tried very hard not to leave anyone out.

"I remember very well something that happened as we were returning from one of the dances. Half way to the college, bursts of giggling could be heard from the back of the bus. After an investigation by our chaperones (and we were very well chaperoned), a young soldier emerged from hiding. The bus driver was ordered to turn around at once and we drove the soldier back to the hospital.

"Other times, on Sundays, we'd take the bus to the hospital where we'd wander around through the wards, talking with the patients, reading and writing letters for them. Most of the men — many were boys really — had been badly hurt and were terribly homesick. Most of the girls had brothers or fathers or boy friends serving overseas, so doing things for the men at Ashford was like doing things for their own loved ones."

Peggy C. Burge was another of the Greenbrier College girls who visited the Army hospital. Although she had been to the Greenbrier several times before the war, when she first saw it as a hospital she was astonished. So much had changed:

Peggy Burge was a visitor to Ashford while a student at the Greenbrier College for Women in nearby Lewisburg, West Virgina.

"I was at the college from September 1944 through May 1946. On designated Sundays, Mrs. Thompson, the president's wife, would load the school's station wagon with eight or nine of us, and head for the hospital. We looked forward to these three-hour visits, and signed up weeks in advance to insure one of the few places. When we arrived we'd go from room to room, chatting with the bedridden fellows. We did anything we could to raise their spirits.

"Then we'd move on to the indoor swimming pool area, where the ambulatory patients would gather. Refreshments would be served, someone would play the piano, and then we'd all join in singing the popular songs of the day. We always left with the feeling that we'd made a few new friends. The experience is something I'll remember and treasure forever."

The Greenbrier College for Women closed in 1972, but for years was a highly respected "girl's school." Its students did much more at Ashford than attend dances: they took part as "farmerettes" in the well-received "Country Fair" held in the hospital gymnasium, their glee club sang in the hospital chapel, and another group presented a play in the hospital's auditorium.

Virginia ("Ginny") Moore lived at home with her parents in Ronceverte, and attended Greenbrier College for Women as a day student in 1944 and 1945:

"I looked forward to the dances. The Red Cross would send a bus (it was really more like a 'stretched' station wagon) to pick us up and take us home. Some dances were formal, and it was great fun to wear long gowns and act very 'grown up'.

"I never dated any of the soldiers at Ashford, as my dad disapproved. He said he knew what they were like, because he'd been a soldier in World War I. Mother suggested having some patients for Sunday dinners, but he preferred that our home be kept private. Things were different in the 1940s. It was a very innocent day and age, and a girl's reputation was of the utmost importance, and my parents were doing all they could to make sure that I was a 'nice girl.' They were very protective of me, and I appreciate to this day everything that they did.

Valentine's Day Dance 1944. Virginia Moore, left center on dance floor with back to camera, was a Greenbrier College for Women student who attended.

"There was an Army band for the dances and they were great! People weren't ever formally introduced. We just all sort of mingled and got together. After several dances, we began to 'look out' for certain people. One of President Roosevelt's cabinet members attended one of the dances. I believe it was Harry Hopkins, but I'm not sure. Here I was, a small town girl, dancing with a member of the the president's cabinet, and was I ever on 'cloud nine'!"

Harry Hopkins was a desperately ill man most of the time he served in the Roosevelt Administration. He came to Ashford to recover from an operation recently performed at the Mayo Clinic. Though he was frail — at 126 pounds, much too thin for a six-footer — one dance would not have exhausted him. His stay aroused some controversy. When critics asked how 'civilian' Hopkins warranted treatment in an Army hospital, a spokesman abruptly ended further discussion by saying bluntly that any authorization by Secretary of War Henry L. Stimson was sufficient.

Joel L. Irwin, an officer-student at the Special Service School in Lexington, Virginia, also met Hopkins while he was receiving treatment at Ashford. Irwin remembers hitchhiking to White Sulphur Springs, and walking along Main Street with two companions:

"We were hailed from the porch of a house by this sickly-looking man wrapped in a shawl. We all went up and talked with him for a time. He said his son, a marine private, had just been killed, and that he'd come to Ashford to recover his health.* He introduced himself as Harry Hopkins."

Hopkins had had severe stomach problems for several years. According to the June 19, 1944, *Sentinel*, he came to Ashford for an "indefinite period of rest," not for any Army medical treatment. While there, Hopkins wrote to General Eisenhower regarding his second son:

I hope you will let Robert go on the invasion whenever it comes off. I am fearful — and I am sure Robert is too — that because one of my other boys had some bad luck in

---

* Hopkins's 18-year-old son, Stephen, was killed in the landings on the Marshall Islands in February, 1944. His son Robert survived combat in Europe and helped found the Harry Hopkins Public Service Institute in Washington, D.C.

the Pacific that Robert's C.O. may be a little hesitant about putting him in. The war is "for keeps" and I want so much to have all my boys where the going is rough.

Lillian Sizemore was born on New Year's Day, 1920, in the community of Organ Cave, West Virginia. When the war came and her husband David went into service, she moved into her parents' house in White Sulphur Springs. Earlier, young Mrs. Sizemore had lost a baby, but she was pregnant again.

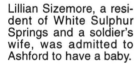
Lillian Sizemore, a resident of White Sulphur Springs and a soldier's wife, was admitted to Ashford to have a baby.

"I was being cared for by Dr. Campton down in Ronceverte. He suspected there might be complications again, and he took me into Ashford at midnight — servicemen's wives were eligible for admission in such circumstances. My baby was stillborn about 3 A.M. I stayed there eleven days, and shared a nice double room with another girl. David, who was then at Camp Maxey, Texas, got an emergency leave to come and be with me. The hospital meals were the same as you'd get anywhere, but I must say the doctors and the nurses were really great.

"Mom and pop and all my sisters at home came to visit. This was in March 1943 and Ashford had a regular little maternity ward. I understand that later on there were lots of births. None of the doctors or nurses appeared to be West Virginians but David's sister, Elsie Coleman, worked at the hospital as a maid. In fact, a whole lot of townspeople worked there in various jobs. I felt right at home."

Happily, Lillian and David Sizemore went on to have four sons, each of whom is a college graduate, and twelve grandchildren. Their oldest son is chief surgeon at a hospital in California. During the war, the "Emergency Maternity and Infant Care" program made the wives of lower-grade enlisted men eligible both for prenatal care, and for postnatal care for children up to age one. Normally such aid would be given in civilian hospitals, but in emergencies could be provided in military hospitals.

At Ashford General, all births were reported in *The Ashford News* under "S-T-O-R-K Arrivals." By early 1945, they began appearing with regularity: from January 1 through February 10, for example, eight girls and one boy were born. Many babies were christened in the hospital chapel. Just three months after the hospital opened, a pediatric clinic was established for the children of the military staff. Part of the Outpatient Department, the clinic initially was open about two hours a week, but later its hours were extended.

Christmas and Easter meant special children's events: the arrival of Santa Claus and his bag of gifts and egg rolls on the spacious hospital lawn. Birthday parties were held throughout the year, and organized games in the lobby were arranged by Red Cross staff. When the weather was good, hide-and-seek could be played around The Greenbrier's famous "Doll House," a miniature cottage that had delighted youngsters and adults alike since 1919. Many patients found the presence of children to be pleasant and reassuring.

Easter in the Doll House, with the Presidential Cottage visible on hill in background. Children loved Ashford's wide expanses.

Elizabeth ("Bettie") Taylor Ballard was secretary to Charleston Mayor D. Boone Dawson, when she was asked by the director of the City Park and Recreation Commission to form a group of young Charleston women to support the war effort in various ways and to entertain servicemen. Though their efforts were centered on West Virginia's capital city area, they also would pay many visits to the patients at Ashford:

"Our first endeavor as an organized group was to hold a series of Sunday afternoon teas at a Charleston mansion that's now an art museum called 'Sunrise.' We had lots of servicemen drop by. We also handed out food to the boys on the troop trains that stopped at the C&O station. There were some Marines at the South Charleston Ordnance Plant, and we had parties and dances down there. The word seemed to get around and we had big crowds of servicemen, whatever we did.

"I signed up most of the first recruits from among girls I knew, then they signed up girls they knew, and so on. The recruits had to be eighteen. Most were unmarried, and most worked. We probably had about seventy-five girls, although they weren't all regulars. We opted to call ourselves the 25th Battalion. There was no particular reason for that, we just thought it sounded kind of military. The whole affair was strictly voluntary. We received no funds from anyone.

"A few of the girls were married, and some had husbands serving overseas. They wanted the opportunity to repay some of the kindness and hospitality extended to their servicemen husbands wherever they went. We took as members only single girls and married women with husbands on active duty.

"I don't recall how it happened that we began attending the weekend dances at Ashford but I think the officer in charge of the hospital's morale services, a Captain Robert Parker, was somehow responsible for the invitation. We made lots of trips to White Sulphur Springs. It took about four hours by train, and sometimes we had to stand. I sat in the aisle on my suitcase on several occasions.

"Sometimes we'd go up on a Friday evening, so we'd be able to go round the wards visiting bedridden men most of the day on Saturday. (Whether we went Friday or Saturday, of course, we came back Sunday.) We were met at the station and shown to rooms in what was probably the Lester Building. There wasn't any air conditioning, but I never felt uncomfortable because the nights were cool.

"Bettie" Taylor established the "25th Battalion," a group of young women from the Charleston area who attended dances at Ashford and visited patients in their rooms.

"We wore long gowns to the dances, and the confusion that resulted from thirty or more women trying to dress in a room with just three mirrors can only be imagined. Making sure we all got ready and arrived at the dance together wasn't easy! We were more meticulous about grooming than many of today's young women, and we wanted the men to see us at our absolute best.

"The music was live, and we had soda pop and punch, and usually some sandwiches and little cakes. There weren't any alcoholic beverages, but then the girls weren't supposed to drink anyway. Although a few smoked, just a little daring in those days, nobody misbehaved. I was single and about the same age, and enjoyed dancing as much as everyone else, but somehow I was the one who played chaperone and made the bed checks.

"There were plenty of mighty sore feet on Sunday mornings, because some of those fellows could dance and some couldn't. And those big heavy G.I. boots could do a lot of damage! We went to church up there, usually in the hospital chapel, but once I went across to the Catholic Church on U.S. 60. After our visits, some of the girls might get letters from some of the boys, and now and then they would come to Charleston. We went to White Sulphur Springs every two months or so for two years. We received no official commendations, but the men were appreciative and thanked us.

"I'm not quite sure when we stopped going to Ashford. It was probably just after the war ended. I know we had a good time and I think the men did, too. But it was about then that my fiancé was discharged, and my interest in the 25th Battalion began to flag. Maybe that is how it was for the other girls as well. We've never had a reunion. Maybe we should."

Laveda Ballard Winkler was a member of the 25th Battalion, and visited Ashford five or six times:

"We went to White Sulphur Springs both by car and train. When we went by car, we all split the cost and contributed our share of gas-rationing coupons. It was a long, twisty trip on U.S. 60, and riding in a rear seat up and down Big Sewell or Gauley Mountain could be somewhat nauseating. If there was any snow or ice, the ride could be dangerous.

"We wore our long gowns because that's what the boys wanted to see. We took suitcases with all our paraphenalia for an overnight stay, so each car would be well loaded down. Most of the dances were held in the Casino. They were always gay and festive occasions, with balloons and paper streamers and other decorations hanging from all of the light fixtures and window frames.

"I met and dated one of the men from the medical detachment. Leon Benedict was a good looking young man from Cadiz, Ohio. Later, he went overseas and we exchanged letters. After the war, we stayed in touch, and have remained good friends."

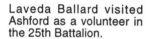

Laveda Ballard visited Ashford as a volunteer in the 25th Battalion.

Fifty years ago, West Virginia's major highways were indeed "twisty." U.S. Route 60 from Charleston to White Sulphur Springs was a good example. For the first thirty miles, the highway followed the curving Kanawha River. Then came steep Gauley Mountain, where the two-lane road ascended and clung precariously to steep hillsides about a thousand feet above the New River Gorge. On that road, a driver could pass the same tall tree three times, looping around it in successive "switchback" curves. With bursts of speed on the infrequent short straightaways farther along, a very fast driver might reach White Sulphur Springs in three hours.

Mildred Foster Walker was another member of Charleston's 25th Battalion. After graduating from high school, she went to Charleston Business College, and during the time she was active with the 25th Battalion, worked as a secretary for the Boy Scouts of America:

"What I remember best about my Ashford experience was how honored I felt to be a part of entertaining and helping the wounded soldiers, and associating with some of the hospital people who cared for them.

"One Christmas season we served as personal shoppers for some of the patients. Rhinestone jewelry was particularly popular that year, so I chose a Rhinestone bracelet for my patient. It was for his girl, and I hope she liked it.

"I never knew much about Ashford General Hospital itself, and the only patients I got to see were the ambulatory ones who attended the dances. I guess I came into more frequent contact with the medical detachment men. They seemed to be mostly men who had been assigned to limited service because of near-sightedness or other minor disabilities. Later in the war, 'limited service' was eliminated and many such men went overseas to serve as medics."

The Army's classification and assignment of men by physical capacity was quite broad. Certain physical and psychiatric standards were set to determine if a man should be inducted, but once inducted, he was classed as either fit for "general service," or fit only for less physically demanding, non-combat roles, which the Army called "limited service." In practice, it was often extremely difficult to judge who was physically capable of enduring combat, and who was not, and in the summer of 1943, "limited service" was abolished.

Ethel-Mae Boatwright Johnson was born in Spencer, grew up in Walton, and graduated from high school in the little town of Clendenin, West Virginia. In 1943-44, she was taking classes at the Charleston School of Commerce, and was recruited into the 25th Battalion. Although she visited Ashford only once, her memory of that trip remains vivid:

"Several of us signed up together. We were encouraged by our business teacher, Miss Effie Bishop, who even out-fitted some of us with her own evening gowns! She lived at an expensive riverfront address overlooking the Kanawha River and invited us there for fittings and try-ons. I hope it isn't immodest to say so, but most of the gals picked to go to Ashford were pretty good-looking. We certainly 'dressed to the nines' for the visit.

"I still remember the excitement during that four-hour train ride to White Sulphur Springs. The dance was in the Ca-sino, and I was scared to death because I couldn't dance. But, of course, when one of the handsome enlisted men came up to ask for a dance I tried really hard. My heart was thumping like mad.

"Afterwards, some of us visited the noncommissioned officers club up on Kate's Mountain. On Sunday morning after church, we went through the wards in groups, hand-ing out candy, gum, and cigarettes to the men. Imagine the impression all this made on a seventeen-year-old from Clendenin, West Virginia! Our visit to Ashford just raced by, and we were headed home before we knew it."

Nila Faye Monk was a young West Virginian from Mer-cer County who, in 1944, went to work in Lewisburg, West Virginia, as a secretary for the Greenbrier County Board of Education. She lived with an aunt whose husband was away in service and who had extra space in her home:

"Groups of us from my Sunday School class went over to the hospital on Wednesday evenings to visit the patients.

We'd play games with them, enjoy some music and dancing, perhaps read and write letters, that sort of thing. We only saw the ambulatory fellows, never went upstairs or off the premises of the main building. We weren't Red Cross volunteers, but it was the Red Cross chapter that arranged everything, such as the little Army bus that picked us up, then took us home.

"We also visited on Sunday afternoons and for special events at holidays. We didn't take gifts or food, but talked with the men about our jobs, our families, and the mutual futures all of us were looking forward to.

"Several of us girls had attended grade school and high school with boys from the area, and we were always alert for familiar faces, but I never saw any. I met one nice boy who'd been enrolled at Virginia Polytechnic Institute. Like me, he was a great reader and loved books and said he used the hospital library a great deal. I guess we'd both have been considered bookworms. I never made any lasting contacts and, in fact, that was discouraged."

A post library was established almost as soon as the first patients began arriving. For the men who were confined to their beds, reading was often the single best way to occupy their time. Miss Alice White of Buckhannon, West Virginia, was employed in early 1943 as the hospital's first trained librarian. In time she would need several assistants. By mid-autumn, a one-room library with 2,200 books and a good selection of magazines and newspapers had been established in the Virginia Wing. Half its books were donated through well-publicized "Victory Book" campaigns in nearby cities; the other half were furnished by the Army itself. Reading matter was circulated to the bedridden in a special little book cart. Anyone else could sit and read in the library or take their selections with them.

Patients' reading tastes ran the gamut from comic books to philosophy. A surprising number wanted technical books so they could study new fields, and be better prepared to find a job back in civilian life. Travel books were popular, and many men enjoyed histories of White Sulphur Springs and The Greenbrier in particular.

The record-holder in terms of the number of books read was Sgt. Stanley Tabery of Allentown, Pennsylvania. Wounded by machine gun fire in the shoulder and both legs, Tabery was in casts and traction for months. Ashford librarian Alice White wrote an article for *The Library Journal* wherein she noted that Tabery already had read 230 books and was still going strong. She also said that most patients preferred local news to world events:

> They are hungry for local news; they swarm around the newspaper racks. "Did the Box Car Bombers win the city league again this year?" "Are Monty Moore and the Merrymakers still playing at the Blue Moon?" "And old Jake got married on his furlough!"

Helen Gainey, from Ronceverte, West Virginia, worked in the Office of Civilian Defense in Lewisburg. During a visit to Ashford, she met her future husband, Dewey Gainey.

"I wasn't immediately impressed, but we started to date and fell in love. He was 'between surgeries,' and had just come back to the hospital from home leave in South Carolina. He had a car and we went dancing or to a movie or just out for a drive somewhere. We double-dated some and I remember one of his buddies dancing up a storm even wearing his leg cast.

"Dewey had enlisted in the Air Corps in 1941, and had been trained as glider pilot. He was later made top turret gunner in a B-17 and before the year ended was in the

South Pacific with his squadron. His plane was shot down over the jungles of New Guinea, where it crashed in the mountains. Though he survived (only he and two others out of an eleven-man crew), he was terribly injured, and totally paralyzed. He lay in a body cast in Australia for eighteen months before they could move him safely.

"My husband — we married in 1944 — was a brilliant man, but the war, and his injury, ruined his chances for college and great success. He never fully recovered, and before his death in 1981, he'd had eighteen major surgeries. Dewey was never completely free of pain."

Ruth Hanf and her brothers, all three of whom were in the service, were from Rochester, New York. Her older brother Frederick W. ("Fred") Hanf had enlisted in the Army before Pearl Harbor. Assigned first to the coast artillery in the Canal Zone, he was transferred to the infantry. Almost at the end of the war, he was hit by a German sniper's bullet and paralyzed from the waist down. Ruth Hanf tells of his suffering, and of hers:

"My brothers and I were foundlings, and since there was no one else to be with Fred, I went down to Ashford myself. My brother was extremely depressed and constantly talking about committing suicide. He said he didn't want to live. He had been a very active man, and he couldn't stand the thought of a lifetime in a wheelchair, and of having to rely on someone else to do things for him.

"I was afraid to leave him, so I took a hotel room in town. For three months I went to the hospital every day. I stayed all day, regardless of the so-called visiting hours. They let me eat with Fred and help them with his physical therapy and everything. I think they were glad for my help, because

Sgt. Frederick W. Hanf with an unidentified
Army Nurse, October 1944, Ashford General
Hospital (courtesy Ruth Hanf Rutter).

they thought it might pull him through. They became so
used to me they sent a staff car to my hotel each morning
to pick me up. I pushed Fred and his wheelchair everywhere: to the swimming pool, the Casino, and often just
some place outside the hospital where we could sit quietly
in the sun.

"He first really started to come around when my fiancé
came down from Rochester and together we persuaded
Fred to go for a drive with us. That seemed to get him interested in life again. We took him to the Eagle's Nest, a nice
restaurant up on a mountain, and he enjoyed that. I started
to feel like I might be able to go home again, and Fred

would be safe. My fiancé and I decided to be married in White Sulphur Springs by a Justice of the Peace, and I became Ruth Rutter.

Sgt. Hanf (l.) with his future brother-in-law, Earl Rutter, his first time in a car since his wounding (courtesy Ruth Rutter).

"I have no fond memories of my time at Ashford. It was horrible. Not only did I have to watch my brother's torment, but being at the hospital all day, usually in and around the paraplegic ward, I saw things that have never, ever left me: totally paralyzed men who couldn't move their arms and legs, one man without arms or legs, other men with parts of their faces missing. God help me, but when you see that for three months, you start thinking to yourself 'maybe it would have better had he died.' My fiancé came in with me a few times, and when we'd leave the hospital, he'd just sit down and cry.

"When Ashford closed, my brother was transferred to McGuire General Hospital in Richmond, Virginia. There he married an Army nurse and lived another sixteen years. Fred was buried in the Richmond National Cemetery in a big military funeral. That was another very bad time for me. None of these things are far from my thoughts even though they happened long ago. I've never returned to White Sulphur Springs. I couldn't stand the memories."

Robert Pearson Lawrence was one of a group of USO artists who visited Army hospitals to sketch willing patients. He had served as an officer in World War I, and sold bonds on Wall Street from 1918 until 1943. Then, at the age of sixty, Lawrence wrote to General George C. Marshall, whom he'd met in 1918, asking him what he could do to help during the war. It was Marshall, remembering Lawrence's artistic skills, who suggested that he become a USO volunteer artist. During the summer of 1944, Lawrence visited seven general hospitals, including Ashford. His daughter, Ann McAlister, has her father's letters to her mother and herself, as well as copies of the 340 portraits he sketched. Lawrence wrote only one letter from Ashford, dated July 19, 1944, but it was quite descriptive:

> The tops in hospitals from a layman's point of view is probably Ashford GH in White Sulphur Springs, W.Va. The famous old hotel (the Greenbrier) was taken over but very few changes have been made. Carpets remain on the floor of the lounges — drapes and furniture are the same — steam tables and serving counters have been placed in the large dining room where all eat except the detachment of men stationed at the post. The bedrooms are the same — but instead of twin beds, there are an average of five beds in each room. . . .
>
> I drew one boy with a very famous name who had been through a good deal of the South Pacific action and was

badly wounded on Munda. He had been in the hospital eight months, yet in his talk there was praise for the care he had received, and he said he was looking forward to the day when he could see the grounds about the hospital.

Another man whose back reminded me of the back of an old time corset as a result of the operations he had. He had been wounded in Iceland and had spent 18 months in bed. The day I drew him he was helped on his feet for the first time and at the end of five minutes he was helped back to bed. "Boy, that's a day's work," he remarked.

From the Valley Forge General Hospital, Lawrence confided only a few weeks later the heartbreak he felt for so many patients but normally was careful to hide:

This place is a test upon my sensibilities and I really have some difficult times and I am convinced I am a poor candidate for medical drawing. There are over 200 blind here and this hospital is known for its work in plastic surgery. . . . I thought I was getting used to seeing wounded in all manner of conditions but these cases are too much for me.

Many of Lawrence's charcoal sketches are haunting. Several are placed throughout this book. His letters and his drawings are yet another confirmation of war's cruel toll. After the casualty statistics had all been collected, the Army placed its World War II total battle casualties at 949,000, including 175,000 killed. The Medical Department can be properly proud of its record: only 3.5 percent of the wounded who reached battalion aid died of their wounds; nearly three out of four wounded men later returned to duty; and but one in four of those who did not return to duty were discharged with a permanent disability — truly remarkable numbers when compared to previous wars.

But such statistics can be misleading. America must never forget the tens of thousands of World War II veterans who still suffer from wounds that are now more than fifty years old.

The final flag-lowering ceremony at Ashford General Hospital, June 30, 1946, drew a large crowd of soldiers and civilians (courtesy The Greenbrier).

Epilogue

At the end of World War II, the armed forces had to decide which army camps, naval bases, and airfields should be kept, and which should not. Ashford General Hospital's commander, General Clyde Beck, who always had shown such dedication to preserving the hotel's nineteenth-century charm, wanted the hospital to be maintained as an Army installation. Many of his senior staff agreed, while others felt that the expense of doing so would be prohibitive.

The overriding consideration for Washington decision-makers was economics. The Geneva Convention required all prisoners of war to be returned home soon after the hostilities ended. The loss to the hospital of this low-cost labor foreshadowed sharply higher operating costs. The departure of the last of Camp Ashford's German prisoners on May 3, 1946, plus drastic postwar Army budget reductions, meant the hospital must be sold.

Before the War Assets Administration could put the property up for sale, however, several things had to be done: the remaining patients moved to other hospitals; doctors, nurses, WACs, and enlisted men transferred or discharged; civilian employees dismissed; the Army-built WAC barracks and gym removed; medical equipment shipped to other installations; and expendable materials either sold, given away, or scrapped.

The disposition of many major items was agreed to in a

June 10, 1946, meeting of representatives from the hospital, the Second Army Command, the Fifth Service Command, the U.S. Corps of Engineers, the Newton D. Baker
General Hospital, and the War Assets Administration. It was
decided that most of the hospital's medical equipment either would be transferred to the VA or sold; that the general
library would be moved to the VA hospital in Richmond and
the medical library sent to Pratt General Hospital in Coral
Gables, Florida; that most reconditioning equipment would
be transferred to Fort Knox, Kentucky; and that certain expendable office supplies would be sent to the Greenbrier
Military School. Well-used Army furniture and equipment,
not worth the cost of transporting elsewhere, would be sold
at auction or through private negotiations.

Then the real question became who would buy the property and for what use? Might there be an end to The
Greenbrier's two-hundred years of southern gentility? *The
History of The Greenbrier* describes the uncertainty of its
future:

> For a few months after the Army's departure, the huge
> white bulk of The Greenbrier sat empty in the summer-
> time green of the West Virginia mountains. No one knew
> what would become of the famous resort property, though
> rumors were rampant. According to one, a Florida gam-
> bling syndicate was preparing to convert the hotel into a
> casino. But because strict Army regulations dictated who
> was eligible to bid for the surplus hospital, priority was
> given to government agencies, local governments and non-
> profit institutions, in that order. At one point the town of
> White Sulphur Springs resolved to purchase the property
> and turn it over to the Chesapeake and Ohio Railway.

Few were more concerned than the town's residents.
They read in the April 26, 1946 issue of *The White Sulphur
Springs Sentinel* that the hospital would close at the end of

June, but that its future was "unknown." Then the May 17, 1946 *Sentinel* carried this story:

> Information received today stated that Houston Young [a Charleston attorney], representing the town of White Sulphur Springs, notified the War Assets Administration yesterday that the town seeks acquisition of the Greenbrier Hotel property, exercising its priority right as a municipality. The town's claim was filed after Brig. General John J. O'Brien, deputy director, informed the Chesapeake and Ohio Railway that the railroad has no priority to reacquire the hotel. . . . The White Sulphur Springs Town Council was unanimous in its opinion that this action was necessary to protect the best interests of the town, the county, and the State.

While watching events carefully, the railroad filed its own notices. It had no intention of waiving any right to claim a priority on the property, and argued that all concerned should agree that the former hotel and its grounds should not be sold for any amount less than its fair market value.

All the same, White Sulphur Springs residents soon read that once the hotel had been appraised, the town planned to issue revenue bonds to finance its purchase. Town residents also learned that the terms of the impending sale would include a cost-free transfer of the hospital airport to the town. West Virginia Governor Clarence Meadows, and West Virginia Senators Harley Kilgore and Chapman W. Revercomb, supported the proposal.

There the matter rested briefly. Meanwhile, the June 21, 1946 *Sentinel* reported that the final hospital patient had been discharged on June 14, and quoted General Clyde Beck's thank-you to its readership and all West Virginians:

> The people of West Virginia have been most generous in donating their time and money for the benefit of the sick and injured soldiers admitted to Ashford General Hospi-

tal. In giving so generously and unselfishly they have made the lives of patients happier and their stay here more enjoyable. On behalf of the patients as well as myself, I take this opportunity of expressing deep gratitude to all of the good people of this State.

In late July, the U.S. Senate, under mounting pressure from many previous owners of commercial property acquired by the armed services, passed an act to permit their repurchase of such properties. President Harry S. Truman signed the act on August 7, 1946. The following week White Sulphur Springs waived its acquisition rights, so long as the town obtained the airport, and the Chesapeake and Ohio Railway agreed to repurchase the hotel. On September 6, 1946, the *Sentinel*'s readers were told that certain preliminary negotiations had been completed and that the railroad could resume "right of entry" to the hotel pending the final paperwork.

In December, largely through the efforts of its Chairman of the Board, Robert R. Young, the C&O repurchased the resort, paying just under the 1942 selling price of $3.3 million, a difference mainly due to the transfer of the airport to the town of White Sulphur Springs. *The History of the Greenbrier* gives Young the praise he rightly deserved:

> Robert R. Young believed in The Greenbrier and in its continuing role as an attraction drawing passengers to the C&O's main line. His determination brought about a spectacular renewal of the war-worn resort. . . . Soon after the railroad's purchase of the abandoned resort, Young hired the noted New York interior decorator, Dorothy Draper, to redecorate the C&O's executive offices and suites in Cleveland's Terminal Tower. Quite pleased with the results, he then asked her to begin refurbishing The Greenbrier.

In what was then the largest redecorating program in the history of the American hotel industry, Draper proceeded to choose and place thirty miles of carpeting, 45,000 yards of expensive fabric, and 15,000 rolls of wallpaper. She also purchased and used some 34,000 new decorative and furniture pieces. The refurbishing took over a year to complete, and cost more than $12.4 million — nearly four times the 1946 repurchase price. Another $65,000 was spent for a four-day reopening party, which *Life* called "the most lavish on-the-house party of the century."

Today, fifty years after its patriotic contribution as the Army's most beautiful World War II hospital, The Greenbrier is more magnificient than ever. Travel experts give the resort their highest ratings.

Unknowing visitors would never suspect that The Greenbrier once had been a World War II hospital. The main buildings, the rows of cottages, and the grounds are relatively unchanged from the way they were in prewar days, while the WAC barracks, the Army-built gymnasium, the Lester Building Annex, and other vestiges of a military occupation are long gone.

But something else is missing, too: the "wheelchair brigade," and the young men sitting in the mountain sunshine laughing and day-dreaming of going home to loved ones. It all seems so long ago, but the young men and those who cared for them have not forgotten that Shangri-La in the Allegheny Mountains — Ashford General Hospital.

References

When I began this book I was determined to avoid excessive footnotes and other academic trappings. But I did include some footnotes, and will add this brief description of major sources. The heart of the book are its oral histories. Most of them result from in-person and/or telephone interviews I conducted between 1992 and 1994. The rest are based on many letters. I used a micro-recorder for all interviews but took notes as a back-up. Few interviews were longer than an hour or shorter than 15-minutes. I exchanged letters and/or talked with most individuals many times over.

All letters and interviews have been edited. I clarified what might be ambiguous or confusing statements and omitted less interesting or repetitive recollections. I rearranged the sequence of some interviews and letters so as to create more readability, and corrected some ungrammatical language, except when it was clearly colloquial or regional in nature. I did not change anyone's meanings. Every quoted individual had a chance to see and to amend statements attributed to him or her. Many found and corrected errors, deleted things that (on second thought) they weren't quite sure of, and often added new material of even more interest.

I made no systematic attempt to verify what I was told. I'm nearly the same age as most of my respondents and well aware that, as so many of them reminded me, it's easy to mis-remember events half a century removed. Still, nothing I heard struck me as impossible or as deliberate enhancement of what really happened, and I am fully content that the stories are as true and trustworthy as the human condition allows.

My next most important source of information was the large number of issues of *The Ashford News* kindly photo-copied and sent to me by Miss Mary Hanna of Covington, Virginia, whose own story of Ashford was one of the first I heard. Later, through an interlibrary loan, I borrowed microfilms of the newspaper from the U.S. Army Military History Institute, in Carlisle, Pennsylvania, in order to read other issues. *The Ashford News* was published twice monthly from February 1943 until June 1946. It was usually four or six pages — though special issues were eight pages — and was well illustrated by staff contributed photos.

The single best source of information about the hospital's organization and statistics — the number of patients and the types of treatment they received, counts of medical and other personnel, the frequency of visitors, and so forth — were the annual reports from the hospital's commandant, Col. Clyde Beck, to the Fifth Service Command headquarters in Ft. Hayes, Columbus, Ohio. These annual reports may be found in National Archives Record Group 112, "Office of the Surgeon General, Army WWII Administrative Records, 1940-1949, 319.1, Unit Annual Reports." At the risk of minimizing Ashford's logistical complexity, I avoided the overuse of these facts and figures. Specialists may dig those out for themselves.

Contemporary newspapers also were helpful, particularly *The White Sulphur Springs Sentinel,* and to a lesser extent, *The Greenbrier Independent.* I scanned all issues of the former from early 1942 through mid-1946, as available on microfilm reels in the West Virginia State Archives in Charleston, WV.

I managed only one year of *The Greenbrier Independent*, kept in bound volumes in the Lewisburg Museum. Stories about the hospital appeared in all southern West Virginia newspapers, and in several out-of-state newspapers such as *The New York Times* and *The Washington Post*. Hundreds of articles about individual patients (and major events at the hospital) were written for the Associated Press by J.W. Benjamin and found their ways into newspapers throughout the country; a set of these articles is in The Greenbrier's Archives, which contain also an extensive collection of photographs of the hospital and various contributed ephemera and memorabilia.

Though this book is, to my knowledge, the only published history of a particular United States Army stateside general hospital, there are various publications that deal generally with hospitals and hospital personnel, and the care of World War II wounded. Among the most useful for me were:

Aynes, Edith A., *From Nightingale to Eagle: An Army Nurse's History*, Prentice-Hall, Englewood Cliffs, NJ, 1973.

Bordley, James III, M.D. and A. McGehee Harvey, M.D., *Two Centuries of American Medicine, 1776-1976*, W.B. Saunders Company, Philadelphia, 1976.

Bulletin of the U.S. Army Medical Department (formerly *The Army Medical Bulletin*), published monthly, 1942-1946, by the Office of the Surgeon General, Washington, DC.

Fine, Leonore and Jesse A. Remington, *The Corps of Engineers: Construction in the United States, United States Army in World War II*, U.S. Army Center of Military History, Washington, DC, 1972.

Hurd, Charles, *The Compact History of the American Red Cross*, Hawthorn Books, Inc., New York, NY, 1959.

Huston, James A., *The Sinews of War: Army Logistics 1775-1953*, U.S. Army Center of Military History, Washington, DC, 1966.

Kennett, Lee, G.I.: *The American Soldier in World War II*, Charles Scribner's Sons, New York, NY, 1987.

Lee, Harriet S. and Myra L. McDaniel, eds., *Army Medical Specialist Corps*, Office of the Surgeon General, Washington, DC, 1968.

McMinn, John H. and Max Levin, eds., *Army Medical Service Personnel in World War II*, Office of the Surgeon General, Washington, DC, 1963.

Parks, Robert J., ed., *Medical Training in World War II*, Office of the Surgeon General, Washington, DC, 1974.

Piemonte, Robert V. and Cindy Gurney, eds., *Highlights in the History of the Army Nurse Corps*, U.S. Army Center of Military History, Washington, DC, 1987.

Red Cross Service Record, Accomplishments of Seven Years, 1939-1946, Office of Program Research, the American National Red Cross, Washington, DC, 1946.

Reis, Hilda, "The Theatre in White: Reconditioning Program in the Armed Forces,"*Theatre Arts*, New York, NY, March, 1945.

Reister, Frank A., Ed., *Medical Statistics in World War II*, Office of the Surgeon General, Washington, DC, 1975.

Schleichkorn, Jay, "Physical Therapy's History in Armed Services Reveals Vision, Leadership," "Early Military Therapists Proceed to Distinguished Careers After Service," and "Male PTs, Established Programs Highlight Modern Military Involvement," 3-part series in *The P.T. Bulletin,* May 26, 1993; June 2, 1993; and June 9, 1993, American Physical Therapy Association, Alexandria, VA.

Smith, Clarence McKittrick, *The Medical Department: Hospitalization and Evacuation, Zone of Interior,* United States Army in World War II, U.S. Army Center of Military History, Washington, DC, 1989.

Treadwell, Mattie E.,*The Women's Army Corps*, U.S. Army Center of Military History, Washington, DC, 1954.

On all matters pertaining to the history of The Green-brier I have found Dr. Robert Conte's finely written and il-lustrated book, *The History of the Greenbrier, America's Resort,* 1989, to be authoritative. *Backward Glance: White Sulphur Springs and Its People,* a random collection of photos (circa 1850 to 1950) assembled and captioned by Debbie Schwarz Simpson with help from John A. Arbogast, was useful in providing insights about the town just before and during Ashford days.

As to the many photographs used: because the original sources of many are uncertain, I have credited them to the persons who loaned them to me. Most of the photos cred-ited to "The Greenbrier," as well as many of those credited to former patients and staff, were taken by the photogra-phers of Ashford's Special Service unit. Those credited to The Greenbrier were donated to The Greenbrier's Archives by the former chief of the Special Service unit, the late Captain Robert A. Parker; extra prints must have been made of many of the Special Service's photos and provided to patients and staff as souvenirs, and have only now been loaned to me for first-time publication. The remaining pho-tos are recognizably amateur snapshots taken by the per-sons to whom they are credited, or by their companions.

Louis E. Keefer was born and raised in Wheeling, West Virginia, served in the Army between 1943 and 1946, and attended Morris Harvey College, West Virginia University, and Yale University. For thirty-five years he was a transportation planner for public agencies in the United States and in several foreign countries, and lectured on transportation subjects at several universities. He contributed extensively to the professional journals in that field, but now writes historical essays for *Goldenseal*, *Timeline*, *Virginia Cavalcade*, *Prologue*, and several other popular magazines. Keefer's previous books are *Scholars in Foxholes: The Story of the Army Specialized Training Program in World War II* (McFarland & Company, Publishers, 1988) and *Italian Prisoners of War in America, 1942-46: Captives or Allies?* (Praeger Press,1992).